# TIMBERFRAME

## INTERIORS

# TIMBERFRAME

## *Interiors*

*Dick Pirozzolo and Linda Corzine*

GIBBS·SMITH
P
PUBLISHER

*Salt Lake City*

Acknowledgments
The authors wish to thank Madeline Searle, whose knowledge, guidance, and support contributed immeasurably to this project.

05 04 03 02 01     5 4 3 2

Published by
Gibbs Smith, Publisher
P.O. Box 667
Layton, Utah  84041

Orders: (1-800) 748-5439
Web site: www.gibbs-smith.com

Edited by Suzanne Taylor
Designed and produced by FORTHGEAR, Inc.
Printed and bound in China

Library of Congress Cataloging-in-Publication Data

Pirozzolo, Dick.
        Timberframe Interiors/by Dick Pirozzolo and Linda Corzine.-1st ed.
                p. cm.
        ISBN 0-87905-970-2
        1. Interior decoration—United States. 2. Wooden-frame houses—United
            States. I. Corzine, Linda. II. Title.

NK2004 .C675 2000
747—dc21                                                    00-026043

# Contents

The Unique Timberframe Home . . . . . . . . . . . . . . . . . . . . . . . . . . . . . . . . . . . . . . I

**The Basics** . . . . . . . . . . . . . . . . . . . . . . . . . . . . . . . . . . . . . . . . . . . . . . . . **7**
  **Color Comes First** . . . . . . . . . . . . . . . . . . . . . . . . . . . . . . . . . . . . . . . 7
    Color Tips from the Pros
    Wood Is a Color
    Pattern: The Interplay of Color
  **Personality: Make It Your Own** . . . . . . . . . . . . . . . . . . . . . . . . . . . . 34
    Contemporary, Traditional, and In-Between
  **What Can Designers Do for You?** . . . . . . . . . . . . . . . . . . . . . . . . . . . 48

**Lighting, Floors, and Windows** . . . . . . . . . . . . . . . . . . . . . . . . . **51**
  **Lighting** . . . . . . . . . . . . . . . . . . . . . . . . . . . . . . . . . . . . . . . . . . . . . . . 51
    Interior
    Exterior
    Step by Step
  **From the Floor Up** . . . . . . . . . . . . . . . . . . . . . . . . . . . . . . . . . . . . . 77
    Wood Flooring
    Wall-to-Wall Carpeting
    Tile
    Oriental Rugs: Artistry for Your Floor
  **Window Treatments** . . . . . . . . . . . . . . . . . . . . . . . . . . . . . . . . . . . 95
    The Hard and Soft Side of Window Treatments

**Special Places** . . . . . . . . . . . . . . . . . . . . . . . . . . . . . . . . . . . . . . . . **103**
  **Furniture Selection and Groupings** . . . . . . . . . . . . . . . . . . . . . . 103
    Foyers
    Hearth Rooms, Great Rooms, or Living Rooms
    Lofts
    Dining Rooms
    Kitchens
    Bedrooms
    Bathrooms

**Putting It All Together** . . . . . . . . . . . . . . . . . . . . . . . . . . . . . . . . 173
  **A Classic Home in Kentucky Horse Country**

**Resources** . . . . . . . . . . . . . . . . . . . . . . . . . . . . . . . . . . . . . . . . . . . . 185

The Unique

# Timberframe Home

Your timberframe or post-and-beam home may have begun its journey in a small shop—hewn by workers in bib overalls using nineteenth-century tools—or it may have started in a modern factory with computer-controlled saws and milling machines turning out the sturdy posts and beams. In some cases, your home may have had a former life as an American barn that is now lovingly restored as a home by craftsmen dedicated to the art and science of preserving America's heritage.

No matter how your home originated, post-and-beam and timberframe (pretty much used interchangeably here) homes offer a unique set of interior-design and décor challenges that must be considered to take full advantage of the interior space and beauty. When the décor and the construction join together to establish a fully integrated look, a timberframe home has an appeal that can be achieved with no other building method.

To successfully meet the challenge, it helps to know a little about how timberframe construction evolved and to look into the reasons why we choose this style for our dream homes. Let's go back to the roots—literally. Imagine the world's first craftsman sitting under a tree, feeling how the soaring trunk lifted his spirits heavenward and noticing the way sturdy branches joined with the trunk at graceful angles to support the crown of leaves that shaded him from sun and protected him from rain. Surely he

*Built by Dutch settlers in upstate New York, this classic American barn has been carefully disassembled, transported, and lovingly restored in southern Connecticut by noted barn authority George Senerchia. Its classic lines, traditional barn-red paint, cupola, and picket fence contribute to its quiet charm. This barn is noteworthy for having a knee wall that increases headroom in the loft, making the space more useful.*

Photo © Dick Pirozzolo

*The custom of placing a fir tree atop a completed timberframe is said to be a way of paying homage to the forests that provide us with shelter. Unlike other building methods where the structure is hidden, the timbers in a post-and-beam home become essential décor elements.*

must have seen the interplay of light among the branches. He discovered the beauty of nature and also learned—perhaps through trial and error—that a house can be as strong and beautiful as a tree.

Unlike medieval castles and other stone structures that required weight-bearing walls to support their roofs, the tree showed the craftsman how to build a frame upon which a thin wall could be applied to enclose the structure. In much the same way, a skyscraper can achieve soaring heights by using a frame or skeleton upon which panels of metal and glass are hung to form a thin skin. The tree showed the craftsman how to get more open space in his home and barns by creating a frame of sturdy vertical posts (the trunk) and supporting horizontal and arching beams (the branches) secured with strong braces placed at forty-five-degree angles. Their grace, lightness, and ability to span big interior spaces—much like a row of trees forming a canopy over a country lane—was far more appealing to the senses than those earlier building methods that depended upon thick, load-bearing walls.

Though we think of timberframe buildings as being made of wood, this enduring technology is also evident in the Gothic cathedrals of stone and mortar. In fact, these edifices were among the visual aids used to reinforce the Pope's message on the merits of Christianity. The churches were built in the shape of the cross, and the parishioners' attention focused on heaven with the help of long, vaulted ceilings supported by gracefully curved beams hewn from masonry. The effect of these stone beams, or branches, joining like hands across the spanned archways was not unlike walking beneath a colonnade of maple trees leading to the steps of a magnificent mansion.

These lessons from nature were passed down through the generations, and, to this day, evidence of early timberframe home construction can still be seen in London and Munich. These homes were built using exposed beams filled in with wattle, or straw, and daub, a mixture of mud and manure that hardened like concrete. When early settlers came to America from England, the Netherlands,

This Dutch-influenced barn loft offers ample headroom, notes George Senerchia, who has restored American barns built from the seventeenth through the twentieth centuries. "As time went on, settlers from different countries began to share their ideas and create an American style that was a synthesis of various European techniques." This sun-drenched space begs to become an artist's studio or a gallery for antiques.

*The angels are in the details of this timberframe, notes barn expert George Senerchia, who carves wood trunnels—a contraction of "tree" and "nail"—using the same methods employed by nineteenth-century craftsmen.*

and Germany, they brought with them their timberframe building skills and tools—and perhaps realized that many of the same principles that applied to building ships that had to withstand storms also applied to building homes.

It wasn't long before America's abundant forests were supplying sawmills to create boards for the exterior shell, clapboards, and shakes. Laths, or thin pieces of board, were applied to the inside surfaces of the beams and covered with horsehair plaster and a final coat of finish plaster or plaster of paris.

Today's timberframe homes benefit from a range of technological and architectural advances that include convenient, energy-efficient windows in every conceivable shape and size, roofing materials that add dimension, and a host of exterior colors, including siding that comes pre-stained for a natural, yet durable, maintenance-free look. Flooring may include planks hewn from old-growth forests, timbers recycled from old mills, or modern floating floors that resist marring and wear.

When it comes to creating a complementary interior look and integrating the design of your home with timberframe elements, the options are numerous—from fabrics to wall coverings, to paints and finishes, to furniture and lighting—the list goes on. With *Timberframe Interiors*, we hope to bring you a little closer to making the right choices for your home and, in so doing, help you to create a home that will please you and your guests for many years to come.

Emphasizing the volume of the interior and its structure, these homeowners used white for the walls and trim and a natural stain for the beams and posts. It creates a blank canvas for a spectrum of treatments.

5

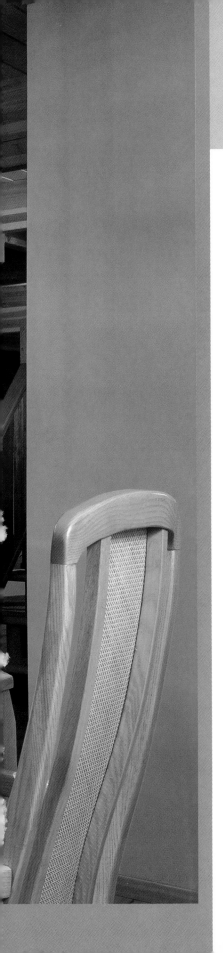

# The Basics

## Color Comes First

Since the posts and beams carry the physical weight of the home, it is all too easy—and safe—to have them carry the entire weight of the décor by finishing them in a natural stain and painting the walls an off-white. The results look fine, and there is nothing wrong with this approach. However, if you want to establish for your new home a theme that has pizzazz and variety, and if you want to take full advantage of the wood structure, start with COLOR. Then every other element—pattern, texture, and balance—will fall into place.

Our relationship with and feelings about color tend to remain as a constant throughout our lives. A little trick designers use when called in to make over a house is to look at the clothes, hair color, complexion, and eye color of the owners. These indicate certain tastes. Just as a wardrobe enhances appearance, color enhances the home environment.

The next step is to determine whether your color preferences run more toward contrast or balance. A few color-wheel basics help to explain how colors work together to select an overall color theme. Primary colors are red, yellow, and blue, and secondary colors are orange, green, and violet. Remarkably, mixing any two of the three primary colors results in the creation of a secondary color that is the complementary color opposite on the color

*Wedgwood blue can take on different looks through the use of various faux painting or creative finishing techniques. Rag rolling, sponging, combing, and glazing are just a few of the choices available. Experiment!*

Photo © Lindal Cedar Homes

*A timberframe home with an added sunroom, constructed with laminated curved beams, makes use of forest green for walls and countertops, which contrasts nicely with the wood tones in the beams and ceiling. Note how well the traditional dining room table and chairs work in a modern glass-and-wood setting.*

wheel of the third, or unmixed, primary. Take, for example, the Christmas colors of red and green. Green is made by mixing the primary colors yellow and blue and has as its complement the remaining primary color, red. It is likewise with the Easter colors of yellow and purple. The primary colors red and blue mix to make purple, which leaves primary yellow as purple's complement. The complement of blue, then, is a mixture of the primaries, yellow and red, which creates orange.

On a color wheel, the primary colors are unadulterated reds, blues, and yellows, often called pure or fully saturated, which means that they could not possibly reflect any more of the specific color or absorb any of the others. Primary colors may be great for color wheels, holiday ornaments, or getting someone's attention when you design a for-sale sign or bumper sticker. Most of us, however, feel pretty uncomfortable in a room painted in saturated primary and secondary colors.

*Though this is a wide-open expanse, color emphasizes the vertical and horizontal surfaces in defining areas. The white kitchen cabinets stand out against a maroon backdrop.*

With the addition of white, saturated colors become lighter and less imposing; the addition of black deepens colors, making them more relaxing to the eye. In television, film, and on the printed page, all colors imaginable are created from the three primaries—magenta, cyan, and yellow, in printer's color parlance—plus black and white, the white being the actual paper.

Even though these principles hold true, interior designers, paint and wallpaper companies, and textile manufacturers have a few more tricks of the trade. These include interesting colors that occur in nature—earth tones such as yellow ochre, burnt sienna, earth red, and natural—or synthetic colors based on nature such as the rich, nearly black indigo or brilliant madder. There are also many more textile colors made available by the discovery of aniline dyes.

With the addition of earth tones, blacks, and combinations of primary colors, primary red can be turned into deep burgundy, and green can be modified to become hunter green. Similarly, with the addition of white and chemically created pigments, tints of primary colors include a wide range of pastel greens named seafoam or spring, and reds such as rhubarb and watermelon. Why do these new colors go so well together? Because even though they differ vastly from their primary cousins, the combinations are based on color-wheel principles that have stood the test of time.

Even if the softest pastel is chosen, a decorating theme based on complementary colors will generally be bold. An interior based on related colors—those

*Earth tones and black—a color, too—add richness to this home office and establish the area as an important place where serious work and discussions take place.*

Photo © Vermont Timberframers

*Note how well the soft green of this dining room coordinates with the*
*yellow wood tones. This comfortable feeling is derived from the fact*
*that yellow and green are adjacent on the color wheel.*

Deep colors turn this
master bedroom into
an elegant retreat.

adjacent on the color wheel, such as red and orange—will tend to be subtler. Another color-wheel example includes blue, which is adjacent to green and violet, and yellow, which is next to orange and green. No matter what tints or shades you create, or how much you get away from primary colors, the principle will hold up. Colors that are opposite are complementary and bolder or more contrasting, while adjacent, related colors tend to be more soothing.

You must not only consider how colors relate but also whether colors are warm or cool. This depends upon the frequency of light they reflect and where they fit into the spectrum. Consider the colors of the spectrum: red, orange, yellow, green, blue, indigo (a cross between blue and violet), and violet. These colors run from low-frequency "hot" red to high-frequency "cold" blue and violet. Hot colors advance while cooler colors recede. A room with warm reds—even though they may be created from subtle earth tones—will have a higher "wow!" factor than a room painted in the cooler blues, which will make the walls recede.

When it comes time for the trip to the paint store, you may become overwhelmed with all the choices. But remember, the basic color-wheel principles still apply—opposite colors on the color wheel are complementary and more contrasting; adjacent colors offer a more coordinated and restful approach, and the spectrum will help you move from warm to cool in the color-selection process.

To further help with the selection of colors, here are some tips on combining colors from professional painters, designers, and artists.

Photo © Vermont Timberframes

*High windows bring light to the upper reaches of this area and keep colors from dulling out.*

## Color Tips from the Pros

Start with the boldest colors first and sally forth fearlessly. Most often, we would not think of painting an entire room purple or barn red. But if doing so seems too daring, remember that those bare walls will be covered by furniture and pictures, and the windows and doors and posts and beams will provide breaks in the overall color. Realize that the walls usually constitute only about half the surface area in a room. For example, a twelve-by-twelve bedroom with two doors and two modest windows will only have about three hundred square feet of wall surface. Compare this to the two hundred and eighty-eight square feet of ceiling—which can be wood, white, or a subtle color—and floor surfaces—which can be covered in natural wood or a complementary carpet. With this in mind, consider how a soft, moss green can elicit a feeling of comfort, how deep indigo can add luxury, or how burgundy can add richness.

Once the main color has been chosen, follow up with secondary colors. When looking over swatches with rows of related tints, hold two swatch strips together and match adjacent tints. This prevents one color from overpowering another.

If you would like to experiment, do what artists do: To keep colors on trim and wall surfaces from fighting, add a dab of the adjacent color to both

*An understated green provides the ideal backdrop for this*

*bathroom's soft window treatment and wall hanging.*

buckets of paint. This softens the starkness that can stem from adjacent complementary colors that leave the viewer feeling a bit unsettled. In fact, if both complementary colors are pure and of equal intensity, they will appear to vibrate where the colors meet. Adding a dab of green to red or red to green will anchor the colors and visually calm them down. The result is a harmonious interplay of color masses and light and shadow.

Experiment using inexpensive poster paints. Keep adding red to green until a brown is achieved. If you really want to have some fun with colors, ask your paint store to create some deeper shades without using any black pigment. Instead of black, use equal parts of complementary colors. The resultant deeper shades of reds, greens, violets, and blues will have a subtle richness and brilliance that cannot be achieved once black is introduced.

Examine an all-white room and notice the varying shades and color shifts created by reflections from furnishings and textiles as well as the interplay of artificial lighting with sunlight from the windows.

The variations are astounding. A rule of thumb: pure white will soon acquire a dirty appearance, so it is best to add a tint following the same principles as with other colors. The trick is to have the paint store make up your tinted white or off-white with little or no black. Experiment. Try combinations of warm white walls with cool white trim for contrast, or, for a coordinated look, try a white with a deep color on the same end of the spectrum. Realize that your environment will tend to gray over time, so start out a little bolder.

## DECORATING TIP

Get an ordinary cardboard carton and paint it on the inside as a way to tell how the colors will play on the ceiling and wall surfaces in a real, full-sized room.

## Wood Is a Color

The most important thing to do when designing the timberframe home is to treat the beams and posts as if they were another color. Although we often think of wood as being beige or brown, in reality, natural wood hues lean more toward the yellows. It is important to consider how beams will cast adjacent shadows and reflect yellow light onto walls and ceiling surfaces. In most cases, the warmth of the wood will go nicely with warmer colors throughout the décor. Instead of going au naturel, experiment with wood finishes that will contrast and coordinate with the colors for the walls and ceiling. Remember that the entire home need not be all the same; some areas can benefit from a pickled look in shades of greens and blues while others can benefit from treating the beams and posts with an almost lacquer-like finish in non-earth whites, reds, and blues.

*A Nantucket summer home makes use of the dimensionality of the beams and posts and the play of subtle shades of white to create an interior of understated beauty befitting the island's Quaker heritage. Notice how the delicate metal gulls stand out against the all-white backdrop.*

Photo © Classic Post & Beam

The ceiling of this home is made of ³/₄-inch solid pine that has been painted white to enhance the sense of height and unify the overall look of the interior. A number of companies, such as Classic Post & Beam, also sell stains and finishing materials specifically formulated for timberframe homes.

## DECORATING TIP

To get a better idea of the actual color of the wood in your home, match it to a paint sample and then use that paint sample to select your other colors. If the grain interferes with your ability to match the color, blur your eyes so that just the color emerges.

Remember that wood absorbs light differently than painted surfaces do. One area to carefully consider during the planning stages is whether a wood ceiling is the ideal solution throughout your home. An all-wood cathedral ceiling with sturdy trusses may make for a dramatic living room, but consider contrasting this with painted ceilings in bedrooms, bathrooms, and other areas of the home. The color can be derived from having a wallboard or plaster ceiling installed, or by simply painting the wood paneling on the ceiling white or a color of your choice.

*Appropriate to its island location, this home is virtually an art gallery showcasing paintings and black-iron sculptures.*

## DECORATING TIP

Jim Nadeau of Classic Post & Beam in York, Maine, suggests raising the ceiling height from the standard seven-and-a-half feet to nine feet in the kitchen, bedrooms, and other rooms that do not have cathedral ceilings. "Doing so increases the volume of the room and adds to the perception of spaciousness at a nominal cost that is far lower than the cost of increasing floor area." In fact, this may increase the entire home cost by only $1,000 to $2,000.

## ARE YOU PROCESS- OR RESULTS-ORIENTED?

Before embarking on your décor project, it helps to understand whether you are a process- or a results-oriented person. After all, décor is a building effort that requires assembling and integrating color, pattern, and mass.

Results-oriented homeowners prefer to work backward from the final result. These homeowners can look at a picture of a finished room and articulate what they like, what they dislike, and what they would change to achieve the result they want. If this is your profile, visit a lot of homes and pore over magazine articles illustrating various styles. Ask yourself what you like about each room, what colors evoke a positive feeling and what colors do not. What makes the room come together? Try to guess where the designer started and what elements were most important. Was it color or was it a commitment to decorate with antiques or create a certain style? Going through this exercise

*An all-white kitchen is a departure from contemporary design and hearkens to the innocent era of the 1950s. The rag rug and old-fashioned, twelve-over-twelve, double-hung window completes the picture.*

A feast for the senses, this timberframe offers roughly woven, lanolin-rich oriental rugs, smooth leather, richly stained wood, and mica lamps. The tactile nature of the generous furnishings increases the visual weight and anchors the pieces to the Gothic-cathedral-influenced interior.

will get your creativity flowing and help you develop original ideas that are based on something within you rather than in the picture.

If you relish the journey, you are a process-oriented person. This means you enjoy the showroom visits to select individual fabrics, finding just the right side chair or the perfect antique lamp. Perhaps you will put all your senses to work, even your sense of smell, as you leaf through fabric books and visit oriental-rug stores, letting the aroma of lanolin and wool waft over you. You may even feel a bit sad when the project is complete because the journey is over.

Kim Wallace, a Boston-area behaviorist and author of *Why People Don't Buy Things,* has studied the famous and not-so-famous to determine their likes and dislikes and how they decide upon the look of their home and the furnishings that will go into it. According to Wallace, people generally fall into three types: the thinker, the visualizer, or the commander. Within these types, decision-making traits are revealed through body language. For example, when making important choices, the thinker gazes at the horizon, presumably because he or she is levelheaded; the commander looks down and to the right, which is where a king's most-trusted advisor sits;

*The visualizer is able to bring together unlikely elements to evoke an overall look. The whimsical soft artwork in a keystone-topped alcove above the mantel is a welcome contrast to the stone.*

and the visualizer looks straight up to the sky, as if he or she needs a clean tablet upon which to assemble the answer.

Wildly successful people tend to possess all three traits, but, in general, such leaders as company presidents and entrepreneurs tend to be commanders—a personality type that relies upon and needs to get along well with others in order to rise to the top. With this in mind, if you feel you fit the profile of a commander, you will be most comfortable seeking out and evaluating the advice of others—including interior-design experts—when planning your décor.

The thinker, on the other hand, wants a logical design. This personality will create a kitchen with a moveable island and derive pleasure in being the first on the block to have the most sophisticated lighting or built-in home stereo. The thinker will walk his or her guests throughout the home, pointing out various technical features of the wood and intricate joinery, taking pride in knowing the historical names of the various parts. If you are a thinker, you may enjoy the logic and theory of how color, pattern, and shapes go together. Thinkers often like music because of its orderly nature and are likely to display artwork and photos of jazz greats who are noted for their precise, intricate, and logical compositions.

The visualizer is generally more process- than results-oriented and has the ability to assemble disparate elements to create something that is new, exciting, and bold. For the visualizer, mixing stripes and plaids is not a design faux pas but a challenge and a delight. A visualizer is likely to have a muted and soft antique rug juxtaposed with a hard-edged

Sometimes favorite activities help define the furniture layout and décor. In this home, several sides of the owner's personality emerge. There are large open areas for greeting guests, comfortable places by the fire, and a game table for reading or playing cards.

25

The bold plaid of this sofa harmonizes well with the accompanying floral toss pillows and chevron pattern of the side chair done in earth tones. The overall effect is to create an environment that says "casual comfort."

steel table and plenty of artwork on the walls. Visualizers tend to like big, bold, colorful prints and objects that blow guests away with their impact. Visualizers believe that abstract paintings, still lifes, and photos of scenery will enhance comfort and provide security. Other visualizer giveaways include larger-than-average mirrors, colorful rich rugs, and a mix of patterns that all work together. A visualizer is likely to make fast decisions and may be apt to change furniture and artwork more frequently than the other personality types.

Commanders love displaying photos of people, for they draw their strength and support from others. Typically, commanders will blur the lines between professional associates and close family or friends. A commander is comfortable inviting his or her accountant and lawyer to a family gathering. Because this personality type admires the role individuals play in team success, commanders tend to enjoy artwork and books that evoke determination and talent. Paintings will likely be of energetic sports activity with lots of texture, like the art of Leroy Neiman, or bronze sculptures of cowboys or regal Native Americans along the lines of Frederic Remington's work. A commander's décor will include coffee-table books on breathtaking feats such as yacht racing or mountain-climbing conquests.

Other commander characteristics or needs to consider are a large foyer, open spaces to entertain lots of people, and soft fabrics that make guests feel comfortable. "One attribute that comes in handy for commanders is that they are tough negotiators and strive for value with every purchase," quips Wallace.

In addition to making selections based on proven color principles, there is one important factor to consider. What is the overall effect you wish to create? Some of us lean toward color schemes that allow the thinker side of our personalities to emerge—the side of us that secretly hopes Saturday-evening dinner guests will cancel so that we can curl up and finish that novel we've been reading.

At other times, our traits as visualizers take over, and we look for the "wow!" factor—an instantaneous reaction that comes the moment guests open the door. Our commander side may be a little subtler, with lots of small meaningful items creating a journey of the senses. Rooms may keep the same color theme but have different tactile objects and textures.

If the visualizer in you dominates, go for one bold color—especially in the foyer and great room. On the other hand, a thinker or nester may see the home as a retreat from the outside world. If this is the case, go with softer more harmonious colors that will enhance your long-term comfort. Commanders are not afraid to reserve special areas of the home for each side of their personality. This is no different from the Victorian-era mansion with its dark, mahogany-paneled library and its pastel-colored drawing room.

You selected a timberframe home because you knew it would be bold and sturdy. Do the same with your color scheme. Your colors should have at least as much impact as your home, so be brave and bold! Then, when you are feeling really brave, go a little bit bolder. Make that red redder or that deep purple a little more saturated. The

This home is a banquet of several textures, patterns in the windowpanes, and color. The scheme is based on complementary color principles. Instead of pure red and green, a softer look is created by using shades that are in the same family, namely maroon and sea-mist green.

29

Note how other elements break the wall space so that its color becomes only part of an overall décor that includes layered window treatments and a richly colored bedspread and bed skirt.

result will be a décor that matches your personality and allows some inner sense of yourself to emerge, creating a place that will be yours for many years to come.

## Pattern: The Interplay of Color

After carefully developing a general color theme, the next step is to turn to pattern, particularly with the larger furniture pieces, such as sofas, that tend to set the tone for the entire home. Again, try to be bold—let the big pieces anchor your theme and make a statement about who you are. The boldness of upholstery, window-treatment fabrics, and wall coverings is determined by how often the complete design repeats itself. A Laura Ashley print with tiny blossoms may have a one-inch repeat, while a huge, Georgia O'Keeffe floral pattern will have a repeat of twenty-four inches or more—a repeat so large, in fact, that a single blossom will take up an entire cushion on a sofa. Imagine the impact!

Paring down pattern and texture can be overwhelming. One way is to start with the boldest, biggest pattern. That is, select a fabric with the largest repeat, one that really pleases you and is evocative. The next step is to select the subtlest pattern to be used in your décor. For example, if your sofa is going to reside in the same room as a delicate Hepplewhite chair, pick a bold pattern for the sofa and a small, subtle pattern—or even a fine silk texture—for the side chair. A small floral or moiré pattern might be all that is needed. This approach establishes a range, and in this case, one that is rather extreme. But it does put limits on the next step, which is to bridge the gap between that large floral pattern on the sofa and the smaller, more subtle pattern on the side chair.

*The impact of this room is derived from bold patterns and almost-full-intensity complementary colors.*

## DECORATING TIP

While a sofa is the obvious place to start in a living room, and a bedspread generally establishes the theme of a bedroom, it isn't always necessarily so. Keep in mind that theme can also be carried out with the introduction of a bold-patterned rug or window treatment.

Be aware that in home décor the aesthetic distances are not the same as with clothing. One does not mix stripes and plaids in an outfit, and that is because the ensemble is viewed from one distance. In a home, however, one sees the sofa and wall covering from different distances, and, though they must work as a totality, there is more leeway in mixing patterns here than with an outfit. A wall-covering pattern that seems enormous when you're looking at swatches diminishes substantially when you view it from the distance of a sofa. This is especially so with timberframe construction where the posts and beams add an element of color, volume, and mass that draws the eye. In general, if a well-thought-out color theme has been established, it is okay to be daring with patterns and break a few rules along the way.

Like good art, interior design must do two things: It must resolve conflict and have an element of surprise. Look carefully at a sculpture in a park or museum. After viewing the piece for a while, you will form a mental image of what the other sides look like. As you move around, you will find that it differs from your expectation, creating conflict and a pleasant surprise. Have some fun with patterns! Break the rules; don't do the expected. Try combinations you might never consider, and create some surprises in your home. You will be paid back many times by living in a home that is truly a work of art.

*This owner began collecting accent pieces long before the home was even in the dreaming stages and had assembled a number of sailboat models, paintings, and sculptures of seabirds. The white covering of the dining room chairs enhances the simple elegance of this setting.*

# Personality: Make It Your Own

Take stock of all the pieces of furniture and memorabilia in your present home. Make a master list of every major item and think long and hard about which pieces to keep and which to discard. Take some photos of the pieces you really like and tack them to a bulletin board to help visualize the items outside of the context of your home. Don't throw anything away until you have made a conscious decision about how the old pieces fit with your vision. Articles of furniture can be used in different contexts. An old bureau in a child's room can get a new life as a sideboard in a breakfast nook or as an alternative place to store gloves and scarves in the mud room. An inherited Victrola or spinning wheel languishing in your attic can, with a little refinishing, be transformed into a fine accent piece for your home.

Cherish items that tell your ancestral or family stories. A display of old milk cans and carrying cases serve as a reminder of the days when one family owned a dairy farm. Consider hobbies and occupations as décor items. In a

This oversized mirror framed in rich mahogany tones anchors the multilevel staircase. The ship's ladder in the background leads to a Widows' Walk, where seamen's wives could watch the harbor for returning vessels during Nantucket's whaling heyday.

*This game room invites everyone to participate. There is plenty of light, and the homeowner opted for something other than traditional green for the pool-table felt. Other family members can read in the same area.*

Photo © Brad Simmons

*By bringing together contemporary, traditional, and country elements, the owners of this home created an eclectic gathering room that is both comfortable and stylish.*

carpenter's house, a set of old woodworking chisels used as a decorating element is a lot more interesting than newly purchased items that have no personal connection. Perhaps someone in your family built model airplanes as a child, and some of the models have survived. These, too, can be displayed in a new context. Even pottery made by children at camp can take on new meaning in the home. Sports gear makes great vignettes: in a golfer's home, place old woods or irons in an umbrella stand; in an angler's home, display antique books on fishing and outdoor life along with a collection of fishing flies.

## DECORATING TIP

In the past, couples resolved their decorating differences by having a study or game room for the man and a kitchen or sewing room for the lady. No more! Couples and families now, more than ever, engage in shared activities, and a home that reflects their mutual hobbies and interests will be more interesting and a true reflection of their family life. With this in mind, even the most formal living rooms can have framed children's art on display or wall arrangements devoted to hobbies.

With an open floor plan defined by activities rather than walls, no one is shut off. Notice how subtly the structure hints at a distinction between the dining area and living room. This enables the cook to prepare food while still enjoying the fire.

Just as we decide upon a theme for our color and pattern, we often feel compelled to decide whether we want our home to be formal, traditional, contemporary, or country. This approach is becoming less rigid as our homes begin to reflect our more informal society. There is a blur between country, traditional, and contemporary, and each style can range from formal to informal.

We are moving toward a more casual lifestyle. People today want a visual link between the kitchen and living areas so that the meal preparation area is not isolated from the dining and living areas. With an emphasis on family activities that involve children, we are likely to have a mix of ages joining together for pizza or chili, followed by movies. Because of this, the TV room has to accommodate that activity, and, in many cases, the ideal solution is to design the TV or entertainment area as a multipurpose room or as a room that blends with the great room.

*An elegant four-poster bed is the focal point of this bedroom, whose country-chic interior is established through a stylish floral wall covering, coordinating comforter, lace curtains, and overstuffed boudoir chair.*

Though we live more informally now, many of us still prefer to have a formal dining room even though it may only be used periodically. If ever there was a room in which form follows function, it is the dining room. The tabletop décor comes first, the chandelier comes second, and the walls and window treatment next. Set up the theme around your china and linens, make the tabletop a work of art, and consider keeping partial place settings on display. Large charger plates—the ones the waiter removes after you are seated in a restaurant—a tablecloth, and napkins can make for a handsome table arrangement.

If your tastes lean toward country décor, this need not be manifest in a corny assemblage of rag rugs and checkered tablecloths that replicate the look of the Waltons' house. Today's country is more sophisticated. It is the look that brings in furnishings from Europe, Mexico, and India. Country style is becoming the look of a prosperous city-dweller's vacation home, not a throwback to pioneer life.

*Simplicity is the cornerstone of good design, especially when it comes to creating a contemporary interior. Note how the old-fashioned goose-down comforter contributes happily to the overall décor in this master bedroom.*

Black leather chairs, a geometric rug, and sharp angles give this home a contemporary flair. The extra stovetop is practical for parties and ideal for families who want to get their guests involved in the cooking.

## Contemporary, Traditional, and In-Between

What do you really want from your home? What do you want to come home to? This can usually be summed up in one word: comfort. Comfort does not dictate a particular style but rather provides an escape from the harsh edges of the outside world. Comfort need not be locked into a strict time period but can fall into the following two camps: contemporary and traditional.

The contemporary look offers more open space, fewer objects, and a greater sense of diagonal sightlines. Modular furniture is indicative of contemporary style. This style ascribes to a philosophy that "less is more." The contemporary lover doesn't fear the unusual and loves the idea of being the first person on the block with a purple sofa. The contemporary style can be surrounded by neon green and rain-slicker yellow—it gets the adrenaline going in a positive way and rejuvenates its inhabitants.

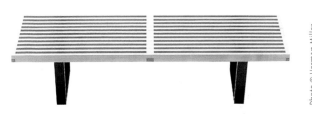

*This platform bench has clean, rectilinear lines and is an example of many of the contemporary furnishings available.*

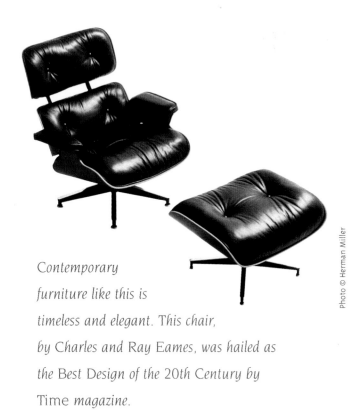

*Contemporary furniture like this is timeless and elegant. This chair, by Charles and Ray Eames, was hailed as the Best Design of the 20th Century by Time magazine.*

Photo © Lindal Cedar Homes

Photo © Herman Miller

Elements from various eras and styles join together to create a personal space and offer a range of tonality, from the deep hues of the sofa to the light wing-backed chair.

44

If your tastes are traditional, you want a softer overall look, with colors being drawn from nature. If you choose red, your inspiration will be a New England barn rather than a Max Factor lipstick. Patterns may include small florals or checks. Traditional need not be cliché. The traditional timberframe home may make use of subtle textures, like some of the more exciting designs of oriental rugs, but in an understated way.

The traditional home builds interest in small steps, delaying the sense of the whole, while a contemporary home envelops the sense of the whole first, with details following.

Within the contemporary and traditional categories there are casual and formal styles. The formal home includes cool colors, smooth surfaces and fabrics, symmetrical arrangements, and plush carpeting. The informal home may have more heavily textured fabrics, wall coverings, and window treatments, as well as warmer colors and larger pieces.

If there is one feature that defines a home as either formal or informal, it is its level of eclecticism. For example, though your home may be cutting-edge contemporary, it may have a plush, red-velvet Victorian sofa as its center of attention.

Today's home styles tend to defy rigid distinctions between traditional and contemporary. Don't let aesthetic guidelines prevail and put style before comfort. Enjoy your surroundings and be comfortable—the only style that really counts is lifestyle.

*Though rooted in colonial style and colors—note the deep green door inspired by casein paints of the eighteenth century—this home incorporates contemporary patterns and colors into the overall theme. The classic Windsor chairs, originally intended for the porch, add another comfort zone.*

# What Can Designers Do for You?

A professional designer can play an important role in helping turn your dream interior into a reality. The time designers spend with you, understanding your personal tastes and relating them to interior design, can be a key to your success.

The designer can also save you time and increase the originality of your home. Designers have access to home products that are not commonly available in retail stores. They can also help narrow the selection process by locating products that will fit into your scheme and budget.

Designers can prepare a formal presentation, showing colors, textures, and materials so that you can see how the pieces come together and how each room in your home will relate to the others. Designers can help you establish a unified, flowing whole. This is especially critical in timberframe homes where sightlines are so open.

Photo © Roger Wade, Riverbend Timber Framing

*In the open floor plan of a timberframe home, look for clues to define living space. A post or the overhang of a loft may be the logical point to shift from the living to the dining area. This space is also defined by the use of an art-deco wall covering that goes perfectly with the Arts & Crafts–style windows.*

Professional designers can also help you avoid costly mistakes by focusing on issues that may be unique to your situation or needs.

What about cost? Designers are compensated in a variety of ways. Some charge by the hour and others charge a percentage of the overall project. There are also some innovative design companies, such as Decorating Den, with designers who are franchisees with access to manufacturers selected by their home office. The local designer provides complimentary service and buys direct from the manufacturers. You pay only for the products purchased.

Designers can develop a personalized plan that is in harmony with your desires and tastes. They can also help to narrow down the field of products, review samples, locate special products, and work within your budget.

# Lighting,

# Floors, and Windows

## Lighting

A timberframer once asked a designer, "When it comes to lighting, where do I start?" The designer replied, "Next evening, hop in your car and drive a mile away. Then turn around and drive home. Pay special attention to how you feel as you round the corner approaching your home, noting when you start to feel 'at home.' Now, you can't pave the way with rose petals or have trumpeters lined up to greet you, but is the view inviting? Does the image of a cozy candlelight dinner pop into your head, or do you want to rush inside to turn on all the lights? Get a fresh look at your home—the look of a first-time guest—and become aware that wherever your home feels cold or unwelcoming, there is a good chance that the problem is poor or inadequate lighting outside and in."

### INTERIOR

When it comes to indoor lighting, most problems stem from an inadequate lighting budget, which is typically too low to accommodate anything but ho-hum brass fixtures from the major building- and home-supply retailers. While it may be nice for every lighting fixture and lamp to be a stunning work of art, even a generous budget for electrical fixtures has limits. It is best to splurge on one or two extraordinary fixtures—one in the dining room and one for the foyer, the

*Well-planned indoor and outdoor lighting not only provide security and safety but welcomes visitors. Note how the structure itself integrates the indoor and outdoor environments.*

51

two areas where permanent fixtures play a central role in décor. If there is a third area where lighting plays a large role it is the kitchen, especially in today's open kitchen, where illumination needs range from no-nonsense, food-preparation lights to attractive, mood-setting dimmers for dining or entertaining. On the opposite end are bedroom ceiling fixtures, which, if needed at all, are probably turned on only when vacuuming.

When considering lighting, keep in mind that today's building codes, in most areas of the country, require wall outlets every six feet. Even though the outlets are well spaced, problems arise once the furniture is in place. Often, outlets and service boxes are not placed where they end up being needed. Planning can eliminate the trouble and expense of hiring an electrician after moving day. In areas where you are even remotely thinking about lighting or electrical service, have the electrician wire the spot with an electrical box. The box can be capped and obscured until fixtures are needed later. Areas for sconces in dining and living rooms, lighting midway up the stairs and in the middle of long hallways, and low-level recessed lighting along a stairway are often overlooked when wiring is being installed.

Two other often-neglected wiring areas are those for mantel sidelights—which help to wash light over the walls and make a room appear larger—and under-cabinet lighting in the kitchen.

*Private areas like this one do not require window treatments and, from the outside, look better without them.*

*Ideal for entertaining, this kitchen features a convenient and well-lit counter for serving. The kitchen is also out of the view of guests seated at the dining room table.*

Where furniture groupings define space, consider installing floor outlets at strategic locations, such as where end tables are likely to be placed. Attractive outlets are available with brass covers so they can be obscured when not in use or when children are around. You might also consider illuminating artwork groupings.

Some lighting professionals advise using fluorescent lighting with electronic ballasts, which produces the same amount of light as other fixtures but operates at higher frequencies, thus consuming less energy. As a bonus, electronic ballasts are lighter, produce less-audible sound, and eliminate flicker.

While fluorescent lamps deliver more light, their incandescent cousins produce warmer light, which tends to be more comforting and flattering. For home offices and hobby rooms, balancing overall fluorescent lighting with incandescent task lamps works nicely and seems to create a more energizing environment.

Unlike paint and patterns, which are fixed, lighting can be adjusted with switches or dimmers to change the mood, tone, and overall feeling, shifting the light of a single area from intimate party, to daytime lighting, to ambient illumination coming through the windows.

Planning ahead for floor outlets makes it possible to have table lamps located in the center of an open area, bringing light to all areas of the living space.

Accent lights installed on the beams enhance the texture of the wood.

## LIGHTING TERMS

Lighting falls into three categories: general lighting, task lighting, and accent lighting.

General lighting provides overall illumination for everyday comfort and safety, fills in dark corners, reduces glare, and adds comfort and warmth. General lighting, including bedroom ceiling fixtures, will benefit from having a dimmer installed.

Task lighting, as the name implies, is needed for activities such as cooking, hobbies, shaving, and applying makeup. Task lighting prevents eye strain. Position task lighting to minimize shadow and glare. To be effective, this kind of lighting should be at least three times more intense than ambient lighting.

Accent lights highlight the color of your furnishings, plants, artwork, and wall hangings, as well as enhance the texture of wood and wall surroundings.

Photo © Rich Frutchey, Timberpeg

*Like the beacon of a lighthouse, good lighting for decks and walkways provides comforting security. Consider the many do-it-yourself options that use nine-volt systems (far less expensive than 120-volt systems) and do not require a licensed electrician for installation.*

## EXTERIOR

Laden with children, grocery bags, and dry cleaning, we usually enter our homes through the side door or garage. Get a fresh look by entering through the front door and look at your home from this vantage point. Does the lighting seem to welcome you? Does it communicate the life and warmth within?

In addition to making your home warmer and more inviting, exterior lighting enhances security and safety. Today there are many choices that go beyond front-door lanterns and a post light by the curb. Much exterior lighting, whether for security or show, is achieved with outdoor floodlights. Halogens are especially effective for their crisp light and long life. Halogen spotlights are excellent for accenting architectural and landscape features.

Arts & Crafts–inspired light fixtures blend perfectly with wooden structural elements and masonry. Choosing sconces or hanging fixtures in the same style unifies the look.

59

*Were it not properly lit, this forest home could feel isolated instead of warm and inviting.*

*This lakeside home's outdoor areas are treated as if they were indoor space, but without walls. Lighting and quality furnishings establish a look that is gaining popularity.*

One solution that contributes to safety and enhances the appearance of your home is down-lighting installed in the eaves. Downlights wash the home in light, accentuate doors, windows, and other architectural details, and contribute to overall security. This is another place that you'll need to think about ahead of time when it comes to the wiring.

Likewise, step lighting and landscape lighting along walkways increase security and enhance the overall dramatic effect of your home. Consider under-stair lighting for porches and decks and uplighting near plantings and trees. Consider strip lights for stairs that provide a band of light.

Doorway lighting fixtures should be appropriate to the size of the door and the façade of the home. Use two fixtures, one on each side of the door, and place the lights slightly above eye level, at about sixty to sixty-six inches from the center of the fixture to the ground.

All-weather plugs on every side of the house are also convenient and allow for greater flexibility when considering what sort of outdoor lighting will make your home warm and appealing.

*Lights high in the eaves and in the pool splash as reflections on the water.*

## STEP BY STEP

### Kitchens and Living Rooms

"Of all the rooms in your home, the kitchen and living room are where you spend the most time with family and friends. Make these rooms even more inviting, comfortable, and functional by choosing lighting that enhances your personal style."

—*GE Lighting Experts*

➤ Ceiling fixtures should illuminate the entire kitchen as well as the insides of cabinets and drawers. Both color-enhancing fluorescent lamps and crisp, clean halogen lighting can make your kitchen the place where friends and family want to gather, whether it's time for dinner or time for homework.

➤ Many designer kitchens feature track or recessed lighting rather than traditional fluorescent fixtures. These are another great way to brighten your kitchen.

➤ Under-cabinet fluorescent fixtures will shed bright, shadowless light on work areas and countertops. They are easy to install, and many models simply plug into existing wall outlets.

*For extra task lighting that is both fun and functional, consider using miniature table lamps on the kitchen counter.*

65

*Installing down-lighting with a dimmer switch makes counters comfortable for informal weeknight dining and useful as additional food-preparation areas.*

➤ Table and floor lamps are excellent sources for ambient and task lighting. Just choose the bulb that best meets your needs, from warm and soft to clean and bright. Remember that you can save energy with compact fluorescents.

➤ Consider track lighting that uses halogen floodlights and spotlights. These offer white light with high-lights that beautifully accent home features. Placing brilliant halogen lamps in recessed and track fixtures is also an excellent way to bring out the rich colors of artwork and furnishings while providing clean, bright general light.

➤ Halogen bulbs over a granite counter are a superb way to bring life to this sturdy material. They also enhance illumination from recessed fixtures.

*Deciding the lighting layout is as important as choosing furnishings and cabinetry.*

Both fluorescent and recessed lights are used to brighten this kitchen.

Since timberframe homes incorporate a lot of wood in the walls and ceiling, make sure light is adequate. Wood tends to absorb more light than painted surfaces do.

*True to its colonial roots, this kitchen utilizes a chandelier appropriate to the era while the task lighting is hidden.*

*Lighting plays a major role in making this open hallway and catwalk a pleasant and welcoming environment instead of a dark tunnel.*

## Stairways and Hallways

Proper lighting can dramatically change the character of narrow stairways and long halls and transform them from dark tunnels into rooms to be enjoyed.

➤ Consider spotlighting a small piece of furniture or a recycling water fountain at the end of a long hall.

➤ Wall sconces and chandeliers sparkle like candlelight when decorative bulbs—available in various shapes and finishes to suit your décor—are installed.

*When planning lighting, don't neglect small tucked-away areas that could benefit from a sconce or electrical outlet. It is easier and less costly to cap a fixture that is not needed than to install one after the project is finished.*

71

## Bedrooms

Lighting choices can make decorating bedrooms more challenging and rewarding.

➤ Bedside table lamps are not only the most popular fixtures for bedroom lighting, but, when used with incandescent bulbs, they lend warmth and create the right mood.

➤ For a bedroom with a ceiling fan, white or clear globes, decorative bulbs, or fan bulbs provide pleasant overall light while complementing the fixture.

➤ Indirect lighting from beams near the ceiling can provide general lighting in bedrooms without the harshness of the old-fashioned, central ceiling fixture.

➤ There are shatter-resistant, Teflon®-coated incandescent bulbs for table lamps that can add an extra measure of safety in children's rooms.

➤ Flame-shaped decorative bulbs will bring the romantic glow of candlelight to traditional wall sconces.

*Appropriate lighting enhances*
*the dimensionality of this*
*antique Herter Brothers bed.*

## Bathrooms

Today's bathrooms are much more stylish and luxurious than those in the past, making lighting even more important.

➤ At the vanity, color-enhanced fluorescent tubes or decorative globes around the mirror, especially the sides, will spread a strong, shadowless light across your face for grooming.

➤ To discreetly light the entire room, try low-wattage reflector bulbs in downlight fixtures or color-enhanced fluorescents to flatter skin tones.

➤ The guest powder room should feature a warm, flattering glow. To achieve this, use incandescents placed in sconces and ceiling lights controlled by dimmer switches.

More advice on lighting can be found on the following companies' Web sites: General Electric; Osram Sylvania; Lowe's; Home Depot; and Progress Lighting.

Wall sconces are the crowning touch in this elegant master bath. Stepping up to a room or space gives it instant importance. The green-and-white tile is a classic technique used to enhance the dramatic effect of this spa.

*The owners of this home chose knotty pine to establish an informal look and to keep the scale of the boards in harmony with the expansiveness of the interior.*

# From the Floor Up

Flooring choices are often dictated by regional customs, such as the predominance of tile in the Southwest. In other areas, wall-to-wall carpeting remains popular. The only products to avoid are those not specifically designed for interior flooring, such as flagstone, which may achieve a nice indoor-outdoor look but has a porosity that makes it difficult to keep clean. Getting furniture to lie flat on flagstone's irregular surface can also be a challenge. Overall, wood tends to be the flooring material of choice in timberframe homes, and the variety of species and available colors is almost infinite.

Whether it's tile, wood, or wall-to-wall carpeting, flooring can be a backdrop for area rugs that add texture and dimension. Remember, the floor is the only surface on which you actually feel texture as you walk barefoot, lounge, or play with children. With this in mind, pay special attention to wood, tile, and carpeting as ways to add subtle tactile notes to your décor.

## WOOD FLOORING

When it comes to wood, nearly every hue under the sun is available—from rich burgundies and forest greens to wisps of whitewash and diverse patterns; there are even wood-tile designs that mimic Italian marble. For homeowners who want to tiptoe into wilder floor colors and designs, innovative companies like Kentucky Wood Floors will create borders or custom images using inlays of exotic species in various colors as highlights.

The most common species are oak, maple, and, to a lesser extent, birch. These are among the hardest and most-durable species readily available. Maple and birch are usually done in a clear finish, while oak is often stained in a variety of hues. One advantage of solid-wood flooring made from three-quarter-inch planks is that the wood can be economically sanded, re-stained, and finished if you tire of the color or want to change décor.

For a floor that makes a statement, consider products developed by large companies such as Harris-Tarkett of Johnson City, Tennessee. Harris-Tarkett introduced pre-finished flooring made from ranch-raised Brazilian cherry in colors ranging from natural to a stunning burgundy that will darken and develop a rich patina over time. This is a great choice for a study, library, den, entertainment area, or foyer.

For installation convenience, both exotic and more common wood species—such as oak, maple, pine, ash, and birch—are available in premanufactured, laminated panels that are one-half inch thick, seven-and-a-half inches wide, and about eight feet long. These floors arrive with backing, wood, and several layers of polyurethane finish already applied and are sometimes referred to as floating floor systems since they are not actually glued down. An underlayment vapor barrier and foam cushion are rolled out; then white glue is applied around the edges of each wood panel before it is laid down. With the chores of nailing, staining, sanding, and finishing eliminated, these flooring systems are the easiest to install for the do-it-yourselfer and result in a durable, dimensionally stable floor.

*Opposite: A lush oriental rug enhances this generous dining area.*

*Below: Carlisle Restoration Lumber in Vermont produces wide-plank flooring milled from old-growth forests or salvaged from Industrial Revolution—era factory buildings.*

Photo © Carlisle Restoration Lumber

Though wide-plank flooring is often thought of as a colonial design solution, consider installing it in a contemporary setting for a look that is crisp, sharp, and light.

For heavy-use areas, Dallas-headquartered BRUCE Hardwood Floors manufactures a highly durable, floating floor system under the trade name Traffic Zone. The product can be installed directly over just about any subflooring material, including oriented strand board, plywood, old vinyl, tile, concrete slabs, and basement floors. The only places for which these wood floors are not recommended are wet areas, such as full bathrooms.

For the traditionalist who wants a distinctive, wide-plank floor, Carlisle Restoration Lumber in Stoddard, New Hampshire, manufactures all of its wood flooring from two sources—aged pine from old factory buildings and old-growth forests. The aged pine is removed from the old buildings and remilled, resulting in a floor with a few worm holes, blemishes, and a patina that enhances interest. The old-growth timber is selectively felled from private land and then air or kiln dried.

While neutral wood tones such as oak or maple continue to be the most prevalent, new color washes of white, celery, and sky blue are gaining in popularity. These, and even bolder colors, can be installed in specific rooms to add interest.

# WALL-TO-WALL CARPETING

Wall-to-wall carpeting is simultaneously a flooring material and imposing decorative element. Consider the following questions when choosing carpet. How is the room going to be used? Will it have heavy or light traffic? Will the room be the center of activity for family and entertaining? Is there direct access from the outside, or will the carpet be away from entrances? Will the carpet receive direct sunlight?

Answers on how to solve problems that arise are available from reputable retailers and organizations such as The Carpet & Rug Institute (CRI), a manufacturers trade organization headquartered in Dalton, Georgia. The CRI points out that performance-rating guidelines are now available for various brands of carpet to help the consumer choose a product that will perform best for every traffic need relative to budget. Most rating systems are based on a five-point scale, with the four or five rating being best for the high-traffic areas. A two or three rating is suitable for areas that receive less traffic.

When selecting a color, consider the impact carpet has and be sure to unite the color with other decorative elements. Remember that lighter colors make the space seem larger, and darker colors make the area seem cozier. There are also practical considerations in color selection. New stain- and soil-resistant carpets make today's lighter-colored varieties much easier to clean, thus allowing more decorating options. Medium and darker colors, tweeds, and textures can help to disguise everyday soil in high-traffic areas.

*Carpeting adds another textural note to a sunroom where a ceramic floor might be the expected choice.*

For high-traffic areas such as halls, stairways, and family rooms, buy the best carpet you can afford. In bedrooms and guest rooms, a medium-grade carpet will provide good service.

Carpet construction describes how the yarn is "tufted," or locked into a backing, and the method used in tufting affects the carpet's texture, durability, and appearance. Pile refers to a carpet's looped, tufted, or cut strands and falls into several categories, each with a distinctive look and feel:

➤ Multi-level loop pile: Usually has two to three different loop heights to create pattern effects. Provides good durability and a casual look.

➤ Cut pile: Loops are cut, leaving individual yarn tufts. Still one of today's most popular constructions, its durability is achieved with factors including the type of fiber, density of tufts, and the amount of twist in the yarn.

➤ Plush or velvet carpeting: Offers a smooth, level surface that creates a formal atmosphere.

➤ Saxony: Smooth, level finish, but pile yarns have more twist so that the yarn ends are visible and create a less-formal look. This pile minimizes footprints.

➤ Cut-and-loop pile: A combination of cut and looped yarns that provides a variety of surface textures, including sculptured effects of squares, chevrons, swirls, etc.

➤ Level loop: Loops are the same height, creating an informal look.

*The contrasting textures between the cool smooth ceramic tile and this loosely woven oriental rug make this floor an exciting visual and tactile experience.*

# TILE

Since tile is made from a mixture of clays and other minerals that have been shaped then fired under high temperatures, it is a natural flooring choice that complements the natural wood in timberframe construction. Tile acts as a unique complement to the natural timbers.

The density and strength of a tile is measured by the amount of water it absorbs. The ceramic-tile industry offers the following guidelines:

➤ Non-vitreous tiles are those that absorb 7 percent or more of their weight in water. These tiles should be used for indoor applications.

➤ Semi-vitreous tiles absorb between 3 and 7 percent water and should be used for indoor applications.

➤ Vitreous tiles absorb 1/2 to 3 percent water and are suited for both indoor and outdoor use.

➤ Impervious tiles are the densest, strongest tiles. They absorb between zero and 1/2 percent of their weight in water and are suitable for both indoor and outdoor applications such as patios.

*Opposite: The lakeside location of this timberframe makes the use of ceramic tile an ideal choice. Add impact by choosing a contrasting grout color.*

*Below: This floor is cool and elegant; however, when choosing a permanent flooring solution, consider regional design solutions before making a final selection.*

# ORIENTAL RUGS: ARTISTRY FOR YOUR FLOOR

Nothing brings a touch of elegance into your timberframe home like oriental rugs, which offer a full range of color and design themes to coordinate perfectly with the natural wood and open feeling that led you to select a timberframe home.

Rug choice is limited only by taste. If your tastes run toward antique carpets but your budget does not, there are reproductions that are given the patina of time through the clever use of dyes, hand-spun yarns, and special washes in herbs and teas. On the other end of the spectrum, rugs with bold geometric patterns, inspired by contemporary American décor, fabrics, and interior-design trends, are now available in a variety of natural earth tones.

There is a connection between timberframing and oriental rugs that makes them great décor companions. Oriental-rug designers are inspired by nature as are timberframers. Both timberframe homes and oriental rugs emphasize the beauty and durability of natural materials.

An example of this is given by John B. Gregorian, oriental-rug merchant and author of *Oriental Rugs of the Silk Route*. He says, "Oriental rugs were first woven in deserts and semi-arid parts of the world where meager plant life is cherished, and where survival depends on maintaining the balance between the earth, water, and animal and plant life. Nomadic rug weavers incorporated this view of the world into rugs that portrayed plants and animals and their relationships in symbolic ways. They also included a healthy dose of talismans and religious icons to protect them and their meager existence from the perils of daily life in such a harsh environment." Gregorian, during a recent tour of his 40,000 square-foot store in Newton

*Wicker furniture and a triptych painting of an oarsman establish a porch-like environment in this loft, while the bright-colored oriental rug defines space and unifies the furniture grouping.*

Lower Falls, Massachusetts, pointed out, "Rugs produced for the ruling classes were also based on nature; except that these weavers used the courtyard garden for their inspiration. The center medallion of a rug is a metaphor for the fountain and the borders are representative of the flower-lined walkways of a formal garden."

Whether choosing an antique or contemporary rug for your timberframe home, use your senses—sight, touch, and even smell. Walk on the rug in bare feet. Feel the fibers with your hand. Smell it. A good rug will have a pleasant, lanolin aroma—avoid those that smell of detergent or too much like a barnyard.

Gregorian also advises, "Look for a rug that is not too perfect, too programmed. Avoid those without variance in the design or pattern. The most enjoyable and gratifying rugs to own are those that find you sitting in your living room five years later saying, 'Wow, I never noticed that little design or how those two colors go together so well.'"

"Above all," says Gregorian, "Look for a rug that speaks to your soul."

## Decorating with Area Rugs in Mind

For a color boost in a natural wood interior, an oriental rug is ideal. Reputable rug companies will allow you to take your rug home and live with it for a period of time before making a purchase.

An owner of a home built by Classic Post & Beam Homes in Connecticut established the foyer as a focal point with double doors surrounded by wood carvings of fish and accented by a bold tribal rug. When guests enter, they are treated to a richly colored work of art set off with an electrifying pattern.

*This accurate reproduction of a rug woven by the Kazak tribes of Central Asia is bold, hard wearing, and reasonably priced, making it ideal for the kitchen.*

Photo © George Riley, Classic Post & Beam

The large leather club chair and ottoman, along with a richly patterned oriental rug, turn this area into a comfortable reading nook.

To make a statement, think big both in rug patterns and furniture pieces. Big furniture pieces are easier to work with when it comes to unifying your rooms, and when furniture is anchored with an oriental rug, it unifies the décor by tying all the elements together.

In a large space, oriental rugs can create separate seating or conversation areas. Jeff Ornstein, founder of J/Brice Design International in Boston, advises homeowners, "Create separate furniture groupings using complementary oriental rugs—a technique that is ideal for the open spaces in timberframe homes."

Some of the most memorable entertaining experiences are those where you invite your guests into the kitchen to help with the cooking. The kitchen is an ideal place for a rug that may have seen better days but has plenty of life left in it. A well-worn rug in the kitchen can create an atmosphere of warmth and unity, making it the place to be for you and your guests.

When it comes to lofts, toss a silk rug or flat-weave kilim over the railing. This will make the loft more private and add a square of color to a large vertical expanse.

For the master bedroom, consider smaller, overlapping rugs to create a cozy, Middle Eastern-tent look that bespeaks a respite from the outside world. This is also a great place for toss pillows sewn from Middle Eastern camel bags.

*The colonial provincial braided rug and American Windsor chairs combine to create farmhouse comfort.*

Black and white are always crisp, clean, and striking, especially against a backdrop of natural wood.

# Window Treatments

Though window treatments are the glory points in any home décor, function must come first. The easiest windows to deal with in a traditional fashion are double-hung windows that open on both the top and bottom. Crank casement or awning windows that roll out and have interior screens are a little more difficult and usually do best with simpler treatments that fit within the frame.

With timberframe homes, the visual impact of window frames and their relationship to the structural posts and beams is an important design element. The question is whether to make the frame part of the décor by confining treatment to inside the dimensions or to go with more traditional drapery that covers over the frames. Consider your need for privacy. Bedrooms and baths will likely have draperies and blinds, not only for privacy but also for room darkening and noise abatement.

In your living room, where window treatments function primarily as decoration, it may be best to incorporate the outside view as part of the décor. If you have a good view, need a lot of natural light, or just like the look of the window, you may prefer a treatment that exposes most of the glass most of the time. A solution offered by large home-improvement chains is a variety of pleated, cellular, and other formerly "decorator" shades and blinds. Look for the newer pleated and cellular shades that can be raised and lowered from either the top or the bottom. This is ideal for bathrooms, where one can keep the bottom window modestly covered while at the same time enjoy the view through the top. In timberframe homes, the wood frame of the windows reinforces the overall framing effect, so pleated shades look great alone or when combined with soft window treatments. Vertical blinds are also excellent for exposing the glass, particularly on sliding-glass doors or on long expanses of glass.

For energy savings, look for products such as WindowQuilt. The insulated fabric of this product runs inside a track that locks out cold and eliminates drafts.

High windows
overlooking
this area bring
natural light
into the room
and illuminate
the ceiling.

## THE HARD AND SOFT SIDE OF WINDOW TREATMENTS

### Hard Window Treatments

Horizontal blinds have been popular for generations, and with good reason. They are attractive, versatile, and available in room-darkening or light-filtering styles.

Blinds are easy to install and are available in a wide range of sizes, materials, and colors. The tilt wand (or cord) allows a great amount of light and view control. Horizontal blinds are available in the traditional two-inch blinds, one-inch mini blinds, or half-inch micro blinds. They can be constructed of wood, aluminum, vinyl, or other synthetic materials made to look like stained or painted wood. Blinds look great alone or when combined with other window treatments, such as valances or cornices. Vertical blinds are suitable in some applications, but they tend to look a bit too office-like for a timberframe home.

Roller shades are about as functional as a window treatment can be. They are made of vinyl or fabric and are available with a straight edge or a decorative edge—like a scallop effect— and with or without applied decorative trim. Although they offer little view control, they do provide excellent privacy and room darkening.

For a look that combines the best of roller shades in a softer mode, consider pleated and cellular shades. The cellular, or honeycomb, variation allows fashion colors on the inside and white on the outside if keeping a uniform look on the exterior is important. Though their insulating value is debatable, when raised, pleated shades create a very narrow stack-up and are a particularly good choice if you want to capture the view.

Roman shades are another alternative that have both the functional and decorative qualities of formal draperies. The look can be as varied as the fabric or materials used.

Shutters, although a bit dated and a pain to clean, provide a clean look that can augment the wood in a timberframe home. Moving the louvers allows the shutters to provide a range of light control, and some of the wider, so-called plantation-style louvers are available in mahogany and other exotic woods.

One approach with shutters is to consider them as open frames into which coordinated fabric inserts can be installed. Although these can be difficult to take down and clean, their durability and appearance can make them an appealing choice.

## Soft Window Treatments

Nothing creates warmth, elegance, and high style like formal draperies in quality fabric. Here is where home fashion and haute couture come together with exciting textures, colors, patterns, fabrics, and shapes. These are a welcome change from minimalist window treatments and a must for at least one or two rooms in the timberframe home. Pleats have come back strong with barrel pleats, reverse pleats, tack pleats, pencil pleats, goblet pleats, and classic pinch pleats.

Tab-top curtains, available in many colors and fabrics, combined with decorative hardware—such as iron, wood, or brass rods, and finials shaped like leaves, twigs, and fleurs-de-lis—are a nice addition

*Large retailers such as Lowe's and Home Depot are making window treatments that were once custom and costly available to the do-it-yourselfer at reasonable prices.*

to the timberframe home. For a bit of city chic, grommet-top curtains offer a soft contemporary look. Oversized grommets at the top are threaded accordion style into soft folds onto a rod. The panels fall straight and traverse by hand. Fabric panels with clip-on hardware also offer a cutting-edge look. The flat or slightly pleated panel hangs from the rod with decorative clip-on rings for a soft, casual look.

Tiers—typically short, single, or multilayered curtains—are often used in bedrooms, kitchens, or bathrooms since the short length functions well in these areas. Tiers can hang straight or be pulled back with fabric ties or decorative hardware, depending upon the look and function you want. These curtains can feature decorative trim such as ruffling, banding, or novelty patterns.

Full-length rod-pocket or pole-top panels are a mainstay in soft treatments and can be constructed with different-sized pockets to accommodate a variety of rod styles. A "header"—created when the pocket begins a few inches below the top of the curtain—provides a soft, ruffled effect when the panel is shirred on the rod.

Sheer curtains help soften the timberframe home. They come in cottons, silks, synthetics, gauze, netting, laces, and even metallics in bronze, pewter, and gold. Apparel fabrics such as rayons, jersey knits, and silky lingerie fabrics make beautiful accents. Duck and denim and lush, thick fabrics such as velvets, quilteds, and chenilles are popular and complement the classic timberframe style. Look for natural fabrics like cottons, silks, and linens—or synthetics that have the look and feel of linen or silk but are easier to care for and clean.

*Colorfully patterned fabrics turn a small loft into a pleasant office or studio area.*

# Special Places

In addition to its sturdy structure, a timberframe home's loveliest feature is its wide-open spaces. When it comes to décor, this feature can also become a challenge, as there are often no walls or sharply defined divisions between rooms.

Before embarking on furniture placement, develop a plan—not along kitchen, living, and dining room lines—that focuses on major and minor functions and how they will serve the requirements of your lifestyle. Consider, for example, the kitchen. The kitchen is no longer just for food preparation by hired hands, but is a place where busy family members can grab a quick bite. When it comes to entertaining, the kitchen also serves as a gathering spot and a place where several guests can join in the cooking. Bedroom functions range from sleeping and romance to entire apartments, baths have become spas, and the home office is no longer just a desk and lamp for writing a few checks—it is a full-fledged professional area linked to the world through the Internet and fax machines. The key to success is to write down how each and every room will be used throughout an entire range of activities and to work with, not against, the structure.

*Left: The addition of a wrought-iron railing can add just a touch of a boundary to make this outdoor space a more inviting gathering spot.*

*Right: This room invites a party, yet the Corinthian columns, sectional sofa, furniture groups, and beams define separate spaces.*

Photo © Deck House, Inc.

# Furniture Selection and Groupings

## FOYERS

A foyer is the place where you want to make a subtle but important statement. Whatever mood you choose for your foyer, try to have threads of that mood woven throughout your house. For example, if you choose a color to make your statement, integrate that color somehow into rooms that are attached to the foyer, such as the hearth room or the dining room. This can be achieved with fabric, paint, rugs, or furnishings.

Many decorators recommend the color green for a front hall because it comes in so many shades and hues. It is also a very compatible color and can easily transfer throughout the rest of the house.

When decorating the foyer, try to think about its use. Aside from greeting and saying good-bye to guests, will this area be used as a place to store outgoing mail and coats and boots? Maybe a small table with a lamp on it could hold the mail. Perhaps a front hall closet and a sitting bench with a nice fabric cushion and storage underneath could hide the plethora of coats, mittens, hats, and boots. Perhaps your foyer is big enough for one of those great antique or family pieces that have no real place in the rest of your house but would make a lovely entrance statement here. In any event, make the room a place to linger, for this is where people get their first and last impression of your home.

The trend in home design is toward more generous and formal foyers, and many timberframe home owners are leading the way by incorporating them into their floor plans.

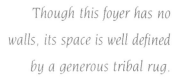

Though this foyer has no walls, its space is well defined by a generous tribal rug.

This area demonstrates just how diverse the furnishing styles can be in the great room, with wrought-iron defining one section and upholstered pieces another.

# HEARTH ROOMS, GREAT ROOMS, OR LIVING ROOMS

No matter the name, the living room, great room, or hearth room is the most public room in the house—the gathering spot for family and friends and the place for celebrating special occasions. This room will typically set the tone for the entire home as it is often the largest and most visible.

In smaller timberframe homes where there is no separate casual room, the living room must take on multiple personalities in order to function well for various events, from quiet evenings at home, to Super Bowl parties, to festive holiday gatherings. You might even use a small table and four chairs to create an extra dining area suitable for entertaining.

When there is not a separate den, consider using an armoire to hide the television so that it does not dominate the environment or become an ever-present focal point.

When furnishing this important room, start with the sofa. This old but sage advice is as valid now as it was when grandma did her parlor. Next, ask yourself how you will use the room. Will it be used on a regular basis? Will it be used as an entertainment area? For family? For business socializing? After you have considered these issues and chosen your sofa, accent it with some chairs.

Photo © Jim Battles

*Subtle maroon, yellow ochre, and green tones in a predominantly natural wood interior combine with a warm fire to create a welcoming glow that makes one want to linger.*

*The literary theme of this room reflects the owner's personality, presence, and passions.*

Wooden side chairs are useful for occasions when a more formal seating arrangement is desired or when plenty of extra chairs are needed for a party. The Shakers had the right idea. They designed chairs that were works of art and hung the extra ones on the walls—relief sculpture with a purpose for the practical-minded Shakers. Wooden side chairs with higher backs and upholstered seats can give the room a structured look that may be required periodically. Wooden side chairs can be pulled out when needed then returned to their out-of-the-way places afterward. These chairs are available in a variety of styles and may have an upholstered seat to coordinate with the fabric of the sofa. If these chairs are not suitable for upholstery, a toss pillow in matching fabric can help coordinate them with the overall theme of the room.

Though starting with the sofa is sound advice, doing so can become overwhelming. Perhaps you have gone to every furniture dealer within five hundred miles and can't find anything that really moves you. In that case, try to think about one other item you know will go in the hearth room: a chair, fabric, color, trim piece, or painting, or an architectural design. Having at least one item selected for the room will get your décor off dead center.

In other cases, just deciding on a color for the walls can help to determine the look of your room. For example, if you have your mind set on red walls, start with the color of your walls and the fabric for your chairs. Then focus on the sofa.

Utilizing the sheer size and volume of its interior space, this timberframe exhibits the "wow" factor in its design. Expansive glass areas and curved braces contribute mightily to a sensational look.

Photo © Rich Frutchey, Vermont Timberframes

109

When furnishing this room, remember that although you loved the delicate Victorian set-tee in your grandmother's home, this may not be the right piece of furniture to lounge on in front of the television—nor would the beautiful cream-colored sofa work for grandkids with sticky hands. In short, try to match your lifestyle with carefully chosen pieces.

## Visual Weight

The expansive nature of rooms in a timberframe home makes it essential to take the volume, or visual weight, of the furniture into account. When a room has a cathedral ceiling and a loft overlooking the living area, delicate furniture on spindly legs will appear to float above the floor. Conversely, more voluminous furniture will anchor the high cathedral ceiling. What is more, furniture with visual heft will help to establish divisions in overall open areas.

The opposite is true when designing furniture for a small room with low ceilings, where more "see-through" furniture will open the space. This can be achieved by using glass-top tables and upholstered pieces with legs, creating an impression of open space. Chain stores like Ikea and Crate & Barrel offer selections of lighter-weight furniture.

It is also important to consider the room's focal points. A timberframe home's hearth room is likely to have a magnificent, handcrafted truss—the color and mass of which must be taken into account when selecting furnishings. Maybe there is a spectacular view seen through a large expanse of glass, specialty windows, or French doors. Either will influence the interior look.

Once the sofa has been selected, the next challenge is to define spaces and their purposes within the room. Remember not to fight the architectural elements that make your home so distinctive. Don't ignore the dominant color of the wood trusses, posts, and beams.

*An old bench from a flea market serves as a coffee table, and pinecones become seasonal decoration in this versatile room. The fireplace is made of Cultured Stone™ applied to the surface of a plywood structure, which is less costly than traditional masonry but has every bit of its impact.*

Photo © Rich Frutchey, Classic Post & Beam

*Mom was right—
start with the sofa and
everything else will
fall into place!*

Photo © Yankee Barn Homes, Inc.

Many hearth rooms in timberframe homes are large enough to allow for two or three intimate seating areas. For example, place two large, comfy, overstuffed chairs in a corner with an ottoman connecting them at the foot. With the help of a tray, the ottoman can double as a tabletop, making it useful for entertaining when it isn't being used for its intended purpose.

If the space is smaller than you like, you can visually enlarge it with natural light and mirrors. Arrange your furniture so that a lot of floor space shows. Don't use rocking chairs and numerous tables, which take up useful sitting space. Use glass-topped coffee tables and open furniture with legs to show space. Don't overcrowd the room; this simply makes it smaller, harder to get around in, and cluttered. In larger timberframe homes the opportunity exists to create at least two conversation areas and perhaps a cozy reading corner that can, with the addition of a side chair, become a third conversation area. Creating these individual spaces, each with a different level of formality and scale, adds interest to the overall room, increases versatility, and makes social occasions more manageable.

Make sure you examine your lifestyle and taste changes. A client once told her decorator she thought she would die if she did not have a white sofa and a formal dining room. But reality struck as she realized that since the room was to be used for a stream of visits from grandchildren, it needed to be more user-friendly.

Once the furniture is established, consider the punctuation of the room—artwork. Art can range from paintings to three-dimensional objects. People used to confine art to paintings, drawings, and sculpture, but now items such as quilts, wall hangings, or even antique birdhouses function as art. A small desk with a chair pulled up to it in the living room can function as three-dimensional art.

*The sharp contrast between the white walls and naturally stained beams is visually exciting and is counterbalanced with a predominantly white décor theme that incorporates wicker. The consistent color of the furnishings anchors the design, giving it a solid feeling.*

The expansive windows open the hearth room to the outdoors, making this modest-sized home feel far more spacious than it is. The light flooring material helps as well.

Use the natural divisions of your home, such as beams and built-in bookshelves, to define areas. Though open, each space can function as a separate unit.

This interior is created with durable twentieth-century materials that are easy to clean as well as kid-friendly.

You may start with color, the sofa, and a favorite piece of furniture. Jeff Ornstein, world-class interior designer in Boston, starts with purpose: "How will the room be used? What sort of conversations will be held? How long will you linger?"

Photo © Timberpeg

## DECORATING TIP—DEFINING SPACE

When it comes to defining large, open space in a timberframe home, interior designer Jeff Ornstein, founder of J/Brice Design International in Boston, has some viable ideas. In addition to designing hotel lobbies around the world, Ornstein's firm has consulted on several timberframe décor projects. "A well-designed great room in a post-and-beam home is a lot like a well-designed hotel lobby in which separate groups of total strangers can engage in intimate conversation and feel perfectly private and comfortable," says Ornstein. He offers the following advice:

➤ Start by identifying different activities to establish spaces within a space that have a sense of purpose. For example, a small desk with a chair and side chair defines an area for keeping up with correspondence but is also ideal for two people to chat. Obvious activities include conversation, informal dining, afternoon tea, brunch, reading, and music.

➤ Other areas can be established for gathering or waiting for family members. A convenient spot for car keys, mail, or a laptop computer can also break up a large area.

continued...

A sunroom calls for careful fabric selection. You might want to choose a fabric that is specially engineered for sun resistance, such as those from the Waverly Sunbrella™ product line. Patio-furniture stores and interior designers can help you access these special-use fabrics.

. . . continued

➤ The layout of pieces on the floor should be echoed in the ceiling. For example, a chandelier should hang over the dining table and a ceiling fan over a conversation area.

➤ Use the posts, beams, and trusses as natural visual cues for individual spaces within the great room and other large areas.

➤ Give every space a focal point using accents such as tapestry, distinctive wall coverings, plants, or paintings.

➤ Most important is lighting. Forget about overhead lighting. In a living area, different activities take place throughout the day that require the lighting to change. To achieve the right effect, fixtures should be at various heights throughout the area. Use table lamps, floor lamps, sconces, pendants, and torchères that cast an upward beam. By manipulating the lighting and light levels, a space can take on a whole range of personalities, any time of day or night.

Photo © Davis Frame Company

*Known as a hammer-truss beam, this magnificent structure is a focal point and a major decorative element. It also plays a key role in defining the use of floor space.*

119

*Timberframe craftsmanship is often paired with the influence of several turn-of-the-century designers such as Gustav Stickley and Harvey Ellis, whose designs relied on simplicity, mortise-and-tenon joinery, and a love of wood.*

*Natural and artificial light make this room inviting both day and night.*

## DECORATING TIP—DESIGNING THE VERSATILE LIVING ROOM

Today's living room has so many jobs to do, it is no wonder that the look and feel of Grandma's parlor is virtually nonexistent. Follow these key points to maximize your living room's versatility:

➤ Look for multiple functions from every piece.

➤ Use nesting tables; they are marvelous space savers and terrific for entertaining.

➤ Make sure there are side chairs close at hand; three people rarely sit together on a sofa.

➤ Avoid love seats; they are generally a poor value.

➤ Keep side chairs in scale with other pieces.

➤ Don't worry about end tables having to match.

➤ Break up large areas with screens.

➤ Show more floor space if the room is small.

➤ Create extra seating with big throw pillows.

➤ Include a round table in a living room to break up the rectangles.

*In addition to selecting the right-sized furniture, consider practicality and wear. Upholstery fabric is frequently rated by the number of "rubs" it can withstand before breaking down. While fabric content and type of weave both contribute to a fabric's durability, price does not necessarily indicate wearability.*

This ice-cream table adds an element of fun and introduces a round shape in an otherwise angular setting.

*Don't let your loft, which is so much a part of the charm of a timberframe home, become a pass-through area. Make it one where guests and family will want to linger.*

## LOFTS

A well-designed loft is a flight of fancy, so let your imagination soar. If you wish, your loft can allow the child in you to emerge by turning this area into a private treehouse nested above the public areas of your home. The posts and beams have already established a treelike environment. Add a futon topped by a well-worn quilt, an old night table with an electrified oil lamp, and a book by Audubon. The stage is set. This is your place to get away while still keeping an eye on family matters taking place down below. Overnight guests of any age will vie for the chance to sleep in your treehouse.

If you have always wanted to paint, use your loft to bring out the artist inside. Since lofts lie tucked under the eaves, set up an easel and create a space that rivals the Paris garret in Puccini's *La Bohème.* If playing music is your passion, make this a music room with a stand, an antique straight-back chair, and a chest for your sheet music.

If mystery novels are your favorite, then a leather club chair, a magnifying glass on the side table and a bookshelf filled with novels from Conan Doyle to John Grisham will make its purpose pop. Install a skylight, add a telescope, and leave out a copy of the *Friendly Stars* by Martha Martin and Donald Menzel to create an observatory. The more a loft is defined by a specific purpose, the

*The Koeppel family of Massachusetts turned this loft into a cozy computer room for the entire family.*

Photo © Rich Frutchey, Classic Post & Beam

## DESIGN TIP

In addition to being a special space in its own right, the loft defines the space beneath it—especially in the open floor plan of a timberframe home. For example, the edge of the loft is a logical transition point between, say, the sitting and dining areas below. Use it to your advantage.

The stairs dividing this generous loft area could have been regarded as a problem, but the owners of this home made excellent use of the stairway as a divider between the reading space and the work space.

Create a theme with the loft and have fun. Lofts are great places to experiment with different looks that can be easily changed.

greater its chance of serving as a special private space. In one case, Connecticut timberframer George Senerchia came up with a unique solution for a client by designing a multipurpose loft in a U shape. One side was devoted to the wife's painting studio; the other side was set up for the husband's photography work. The connecting area, the bottom part of the U, was where the children played. Everyone got a defined space for their specific activities, yet they could all be together, working and playing, without intruding on each other's projects.

Photo © Roger Wade, Riverbend Timber Framing

A three-inch-thick foam
cushion and lots of comfy
throw pillows transform an
ordinary window seat into
an inviting special place.

*The dining room may only be used for Sunday dinner, or even less frequently, but it should not become a catchall for homework papers, junk mail, and other family flotsam.*

## DINING ROOMS

Many homeowners treat their dining room much more formally, making this room entirely distinct from the rest of the home and its more relaxed décor. Perhaps this is because the dining room is where families celebrate holidays with religious significance and life's great passages, such as birthdays, wedding anniversaries, and graduation.

Since form follows function, be sure to consider food presentation as an actual design element. This includes the china, crystal, silverware, and table linens, all of which play a role in setting the tone of the room. The dining room should titillate the senses.

When selecting a table for the dining room, consider how it will look set with a full range of wares, from everyday to grandmother's fine bone china. In many cases, leaving the table set up to accommodate a romantic dinner for two can add interest and warmth. It can also prevent family members from using the dining room table as a catchall. At other times, pizza parties may be more typical,

In homes where the majority of the wood is lighter, choose a traditional mahogany table and chairs and an elegant chandelier to create a surprise and make the dining room special.

## DECORATING TIP—DEFINING SPACE IN THE DINING ROOM

At the flooring stage, consider defining the space with a border that goes around the perimeter of the room. When laying flooring, ask about decorative strips in a contrasting hardwood, such as mahogany with oak or maple. Tile also offers these options.

but a very informal dining room can be dressed up with linens, candelabras, and tabletop decorations for formal occasions such as Christmas or Thanksgiving dinner.

Buffet and service tops are perfect for display. Consider an interesting shelf of granite or an old piece of wood mounted on columns or with brackets.

The dining room rug is key. The most common mistake is not getting a big-enough rug. When you are seated at the table, all seats should be on the rug, but don't worry if the chairs go past the rug when you leave the table.

With a glass-top table, consider a medallion rug. A strong border on the rug makes for a nice contrast. As far as layout, it's tough to be original with a dining room. The focus is the table with all

*Simplicity is the byword of this dining room, yet the colorful rug adds a measure of whimsy.*

Photo © Deck House, Inc.

*The combination of a cherry table and black chairs is both stunning and warm.*

directional elements leading your eye toward the center of the table. Since the lighting fixture dictates placement of furniture, consider using three pendant lights instead of the customary chandelier.

If you have ordinary-height ceilings in the dining room, stick with a one-tier chandelier. If you have a cathedral ceiling, then go with a double or triple-tier chandelier. A downlight in the center of the chandelier is a wonderful way to soften the look of the dining room or to simply showcase a nice floral centerpiece when the room is not in use.

## DECORATING TIP

Since the dining room is designed for guests to be seated, hang artwork slightly lower than in other rooms.

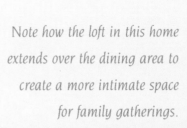

*Note how the loft in this home extends over the dining area to create a more intimate space for family gatherings.*

Photo © Vermont Timberframes

## DECORATING TIP

A dark-colored tablecloth makes crystal and china pop. The same principle is behind the practice of displaying diamond rings and jewelry on black velvet. Be sure to use a custom table pad to protect the table's surface against everyday perils.

*A timberframe home need not be decorated in classic style. The style of this dining room set and the architectural windows are reminiscent of 1920s modernism.*

# KITCHENS

When cabinets, appliances, and décor elements such as countertops and flooring are considered, the kitchen can be the most difficult and expensive room in the house to decorate. Remember that this is the only room in which the bulk of the design decisions cannot be easily revised, since the overall look and style is literally built in with cabinetry and appliances.

The first step—even prior to budgeting—is to consider your own culinary habits and how much use the kitchen will actually receive. Kitchen users range from couples for whom every meal is a culinary adventure to those who don't want to make anything more complicated than dinner reservations. And keep in mind that a summer-home kitchen will only receive two to three months of use per year, so budget-priced appliances may be more than adequate.

One should remember resale value when considering décor extremes. While the master chef may be comfortable in a professional restaurant kitchen, others may find all the stainless steel a little off-putting. Conversely, homeowners who have installed galley kitchens in relatively large homes often find the space inadequate for meal preparation.

*An ideal setting for intimate weeknight dining for two. In some cases, a drop-leaf table can be placed near a window for casual meals and moved to the center for more formal occasions. The sideboard adds interest and convenience.*

Photo © Roger Wade, Riverbend Timber Framing

One professional architect looks at kitchens this way: "Imagination and flexibility are key to a successful design," says Alex Anamiahian of Anamiahian Winton Architects in Cambridge, Massachusetts. Anamiahian continues, "A kitchen can be like a giant puzzle. The pieces are the cabinets, appliances, and the walls. The budget defines the perimeter. Don't expect every piece to fit correctly the first time you try it on graph paper."

Seek the advice of kitchen-design professionals—they will see opportunities to meet your needs that even the best builders, designers, and architects miss. It is also important to shop around. There is a wide range of cabinetry available, from custom to mass-produced, and even ready-to-assemble (RTA) units for the budget minded.

Kitchen cabinetry is now being treated more like furniture, with pieces resembling a collection of china closets, Hoosier cabinets, and grain bins, which, according to David Leonard, cofounder of the Kennebec Company in Bath, Maine, were standard pieces in kitchens long ago. Leonard started his kitchen-design and custom-manufacturing company out of a love of American architecture. He notes, "Though we create a look reminiscent of the past, we do so with contemporary family life in mind."

*When considered as whole elements, the cabinets, countertops, flooring, and furnishings can work together to complement the timberframe beams.*

Photo © Davis Frame Company

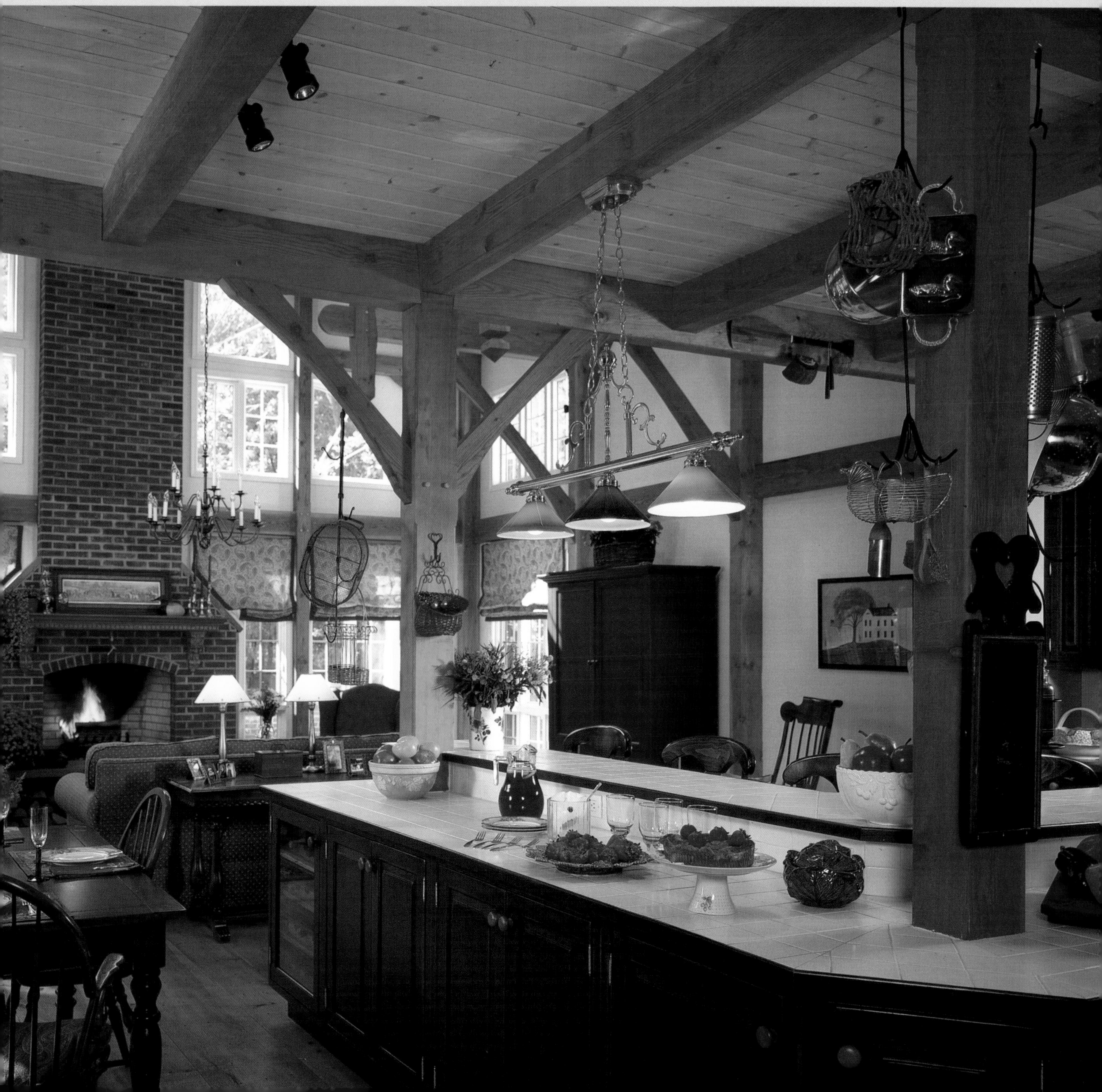

*This kitchen's generous counter space will accommodate a family of cooks and ambitious gourmet-meal preparation.*

The Kennebec Company was so successful that it attracted the attention of *This Old House* when it was restoring the Weatherbee Farm, a two-hundred-year-old timberframe farmhouse in Westwood, Massachusetts. *This Old House* credited Kennebec for cabinetry that "preserves the house's integrity as a piece of American history, while sensitively rebuilding a modern, functional space to meet the needs of twentieth-century homeowners with growing families." Kennebec achieved this feeling by designing individual pieces that appear to have been added by successive generations of Weatherbee farm families. Special enclosures were also created for the ovens and refrigerator to keep intact the original eighteenth-century charm.

There are many other dimensions to consider. The space around islands must be at least forty-two inches, otherwise the kitchen will feel cramped. If the island has a cook top, it must be inset by six inches so that pot handles won't extend over the counter's edge and tempt toddlers. Snack-bar counters must be at least a foot deep and two feet wide for every person you want to accommodate or the family will be eating in shifts.

One of the biggest misconceptions is that base cabinets must line up with wall cabinets size-for-size and box-for-box. Just because a base cabinet is thirty-three inches wide, you don't have to install corresponding wall cabinets of the same width. Doing so not only costs more but is unattractive as well.

*The owner of this home bought an old grain bin to provide the convenience of a movable island with maximum versatility.*

Consider mass merchandisers such as Lowe's and Home Depot, which can be valuable sources for a range of cabinetry quality and prices. Home Depot's larger stores have a kitchen-cabinet center, complete with several models on display, professional designers, and computer programs that provide layouts and virtual kitchens in 3-D. There are also plenty of informative signs so that the consumer can do some comparison shopping before speaking with a designer. The signs compare price levels for ten-by-ten-foot kitchen spaces in a range of cabinetry. With some patience and the ability to follow directions, any do-it-yourselfer can save a bundle by putting these cabinet kits together.

Make sure there is adequate task lighting, which can include small decorative lamps placed on the counters. For overall lighting, consider banks of recessed lights on separate dimmers to create a variety of moods.

Whether you're a high-end or budget-minded consumer, it is best to do plenty of shopping, and, since you'll be spending a lot of time together, look for a kitchen-cabinet and design company with which you have the right chemistry. One of the best ways to get started is to contact the National Kitchen & Bath Association at 800-FOR NKBA. Ask for the NKBA's do-it-yourself remodeling organizer, *The Little Book of Kitchen and Bath Wisdom*, and a list of retailers and manufacturers who are members of the association.

*A professional stove is not only attractive but also practical for the culinary buff.*

*This kitchen has a powerful overall theme. The additional cabinetry visually divides the food-preparation area and creates a convenient and attractive place for serving and storing dinnerware.*

## DECORATING TIPS—KITCHEN

➤ In keeping with the concept of cabinets as furniture, consider a secondhand desk as a work area.

➤ For linen storage, look around for old retail display cabinets, which your kitchen-cabinet designer can incorporate into the overall design.

➤ Have multilevel work surfaces.

➤ Establish a working-cook's kitchen with a Peg-Board™ to keep utensils close at hand.

➤ Keep dishes out of the sink with the help of two dishwashers. The newer dishwasher drawer appliances are a unique place for glasses and can be installed in the great room for those who frequently entertain.

➤ Enjoy the convenience of two or three smaller refrigerators, strategically placed; this can prove especially handy for avid cooks.

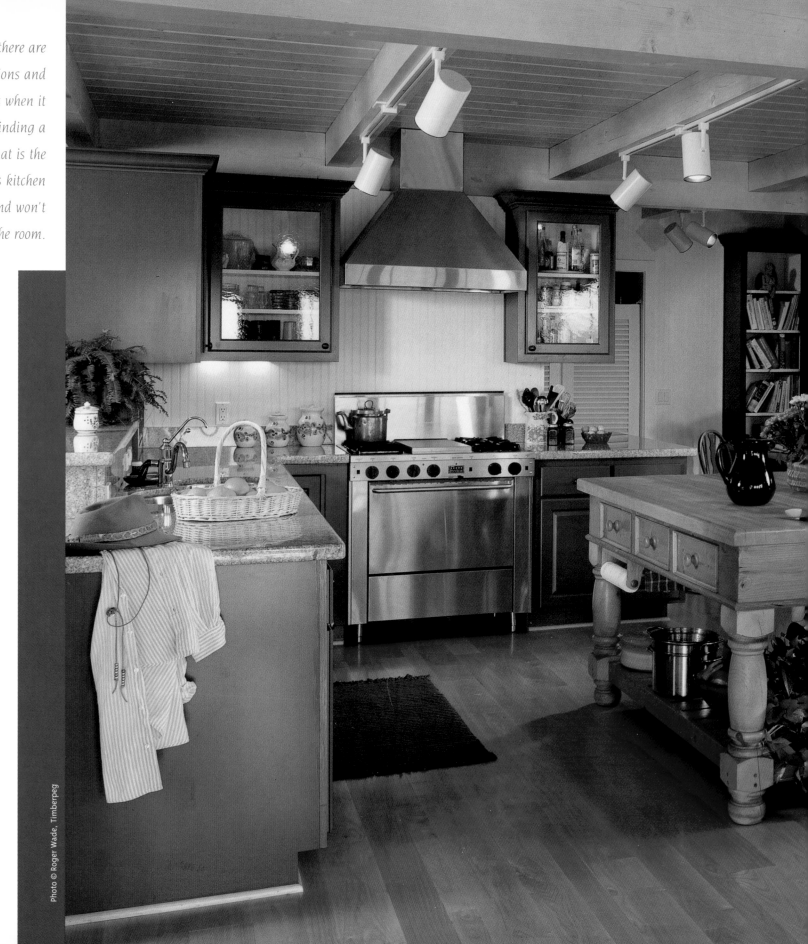

Today there are greater selections and price ranges when it comes to finding a refrigerator that is the same depth as kitchen counters and won't stick out into the room.

## DECORATING TIPS—KITCHEN ADVICE FROM A TIMBER HOME EXPERT

Jim Nadeau of Classic Post & Beam in York, Maine, offers this kitchen-design advice from his unique vantage point as a representative of a leading manufacturer of post-and-beam homes.

➤ If you can see the cabinet tops from a loft or stair landing, the tops should be finished with the same material and care as the cabinet faces.

➤ Insist on having the kitchen designer visit the job site and take measurements of the actual space, including the location and size of the posts. Manufacturing cabinets at the factory that fit properly is less costly than altering them on the job site.

➤ Timberframe manufacturers will provide a basic kitchen layout, indicating the location of sinks, ranges, refrigerators, dishwashers, and other appliances. The easiest installation is to have the cabinets butt up to the face of the posts and leave a space behind the cabinets for extra shelves. While planning your kitchen, your best bet is to ask the kitchen designer to coordinate with the builder.

➤ Remind your kitchen designer that the exterior walls will likely be constructed of solid, stress-skin panels. Interior walls will be built using two-by-four-inch studs.

➤ Consider skylights and plenty of recessed or track lighting to brighten your kitchen and work areas.

➤ Contrast your cabinets with other wood in the home. Consider using wood species different from your beams; try pickled finishes, or even cabinets done in bold colors—all of these will add interest.

➤ Allow space to display pictures, collections, antiques, plants, and other items to personalize your kitchen as you would any other room in your new home.

Though the over-the-sink window is obligatory, don't be afraid to order an extra-large window. You might sacrifice some cabinet space, but this will be more than made up for with the additional natural light and pleasantness of the room.

Photo © Brad Simmons

## DECORATING TIPS—KITCHEN ADVICE FROM A KITCHEN-DESIGN COMPANY

David Leonard, co-founder of the Kennebec Company in Bath, Maine, offers this kitchen-design advice.

➤ The well-designed kitchen does not use filler spaces.

➤ Don't over-accessorize. Accessories can restrict cabinetry use, which may impede the function and efficiency of the kitchen.

➤ Consider a walk-in pantry. Pantries can store bulky items and can be useful for the homeowner who buys food in large quantities. Also, open shelving is less costly than cabinets. The one door to the pantry can be closed to effectively eliminate kitchen clutter.

➤ The efficiency of the kitchen is what matters—not the amount of storage space. Don't pay for expensive cabinets to store items you use only on occasion. Use other areas such as a walk-in pantry or closet to store seldom-used items. Give away the stuff that you don't use.

➤ Islands are useful but only when space allows. These workspaces need at least forty-two inches all around to accommodate the flow of traffic.

➤ Attempt to show as much of the timberframe structure as possible by confining cabinetry to less architecturally interesting areas.

*A skylight can add light and texture to the kitchen.*

When it comes to planning and installing kitchen cabinets, encourage communication among your kitchen designer, timberframe company, and architect. It is best to take final measurements on-site after the posts and beams are in place and the walls and windows are installed.

Don't sacrifice function for fun when you can have both. Accessorize with lively objects like these bright chrome diner stools.

## BEDROOMS

### Master Bedrooms

The bedroom is the crown of the home and an escape from the world. This is a romantic room that bespeaks luxury, warmth, and sex appeal.

While rules are made to be broken, the cardinal rule of good bedroom design is to situate the headboard on the wall opposite the entry, if at all possible. This way, when people enter, they get the full impact.

On the more luxurious end are canopy beds, which help add visual weight to a room, especially if there is a cathedral ceiling. Consider additional seating, such as a chaise lounge, to enhance the level of elegance and romance in the master bedroom.

Give life to the bed by making it a flight of fancy. Pile on the down comforter, and focus on fluff rather than structure. Go wild with bed skirts. Newer mattresses result in a higher bed, which adds to the sense of elegance.

Bedrooms by tradition resist eclecticism. The key is to have some fun by choosing a headboard of contrasting material, such as rough-hewn board or wrought iron, to give the room an element of surprise. For an added touch, go with footboards. Create interest with mirrors, and remember that night tables do not have to match. Consider using a huge armoire for hanging clothes.

*Opposite: With the sights and sounds of the ocean to wake up to, consider a minimalist interior that does nothing to distract from the show going on at center stage.*

*Below: Give life to the bedroom by making the bed a flight of fancy. This ornate wrought-iron bed with lots of pillows, combined with a tasteful window treatment and colorful rug, makes an inviting escape.*

Photo © Jim Battles

151

## DECORATING TIPS—BEDROOMS

➤ Use a dresser top as a place for additional lighting.

➤ Put lighting in the armoire; it may be a great help for finding socks that match.

➤ Install dimmers on every light—even table lamps—so that you can control the mood.

➤ Include plants to soften corners and prevent clothes pileups.

➤ Hang art lower and near the bed.

➤ Display personal mementos on a nightstand.

➤ Bring the ceiling down with a shelf about six feet off the floor to display rare books and memorabilia.

➤ Paint high ceilings a shade darker than the walls.

➤ Give window treatments special attention. Even if you don't need privacy, bedroom windows without drapery are black holes at night.

The master bedroom is becoming a suite— a getaway—where the boudoir chair is more than a clothes rack; it's also a place to enjoy a good book or keep up with correspondence. The layout separates the sleeping and reading areas to reinforce this feeling.

*Shaker simplicity speaks volumes in this bedroom, inspired by the religious movement that brought us such practical items as clothespins and seed packages.*

## Children's Rooms

The décor has to change as fast as the kids do. Stay flexible and as the kids grow, let them have a hand in the design decisions—after all, this is their retreat. Consider decorating with their favorite hobbies or characters in mind.

Special note: Nurseries today are becoming more upscale, with professionally coordinated decorations and furnishings available in most baby stores. Go this route if you have the resources, but don't get swept up into a costly décor that will be satisfying for only a year or so.

## DECORATING TIP

Hard-wire children's rooms for cable television, phones, intercom, Internet, and all the trappings of technology before you actually need it. It won't be long before the need for an intercom in the nursery will give way to the need for a computer in a homework and study area or home office.

A fireplace and
deck make this
multipurpose suite
a wonderful place
to be in every season.

The ceiling fan in this bedroom is manufactured of bent fishing rods, sailcloth, and fishing line to underscore the lakeside theme. The massive bedposts contribute to a look that is reminiscent of summer camp.

The wingback chair, dresser, and quilt give this room the feeling of a Vermont country inn.

The pristine white-and-blue
décor with lots of windows
trimmed in a foliage motif
makes this room light, airy, and
appealing to overnight guests.

## BATHROOMS

Go lavish. Take your bath budget and double it. After all, exotic tile can last a lifetime and quality fixtures will remain in vogue for decades. Consider the retro look and how sought after claw-foot tubs are today. And, if you want, make your master suite an apartment within your home; create a bath that functions as a spa. Utilize the ideas on the following page when planning your bathroom.

*With stress being the byword of modern living, the bath has become the personal spa for getting away from the world. Step-up architecture adds to the feeling of elegance.*

*Though modest in size, the oriental rug adds a vital touch of elegance to this bath and will withstand the rigors of moisture for decades.*

*Opposite: Step up and take in the view from this oversized built-in bathtub with separate shower.*

## DECORATING TIP—BATHROOMS

➤ Fixtures and tile last a lifetime. The safe bet is to go with a neutral look. Items such as wallpaper, towels, and bath accessories will accent with color and add excitement.

➤ Lay tiles on the diagonal and use large tiles. Instead of making a color statement with permanent tile, emphasize texture, pattern, and decorative molding. The natural look of tile goes well with the overall feeling of a timberframe home. Variations in the sheen of the glazing can also add interest.

➤ Bathrooms should reflect and complement the style of the rest of the house.

➤ The bathroom is a natural place for a plant and a piece of furniture such as a chair. Build your vanity on legs or make it look like an antique washstand.

➤ In a small bathroom, a pedestal sink looks best because it does not intrude on the floor space. Use a small container or cabinet for your health and beauty aids.

➤ Framed mirrors add a touch of elegance and are more becoming than wall mirrors that seem suspended in space.

➤ If you are going to have built-ins, they should go flush with the beams so you don't have to interrupt the counter. Built-ins are great for displaying plants as well as cosmetics, shampoos, bath

continued...

*Vanity sidelights work well
when added light is needed
for applying makeup.*

Photo © Lindal Cedar Homes

...continued

salts, and soaps that are often attractive left in their own wrapping. Install plenty of hooks for robes, extra towels, and hair dryers.

➤ Don't forget to integrate artwork into the bathroom. This is what really makes the bath look and feel like a real room. Select pieces that can withstand the humidity. For example, rather than featuring an original watercolor, try poster art or a print that does not cost a fortune. And, of course, sculptures and relaxing fountains are always nice accents for a bathroom.

➤ Plan your electrical outlets in advance so that lamps can be placed in the bathroom. A nice little lamp keyed to the switch is ideal. Extra outlets also help to accommodate appliances.

➤ Don't hide towels behind a linen-closet door. Fold them up and display them on open shelves or in baskets to add soft notes to the cold porcelain, brass, or chrome fixtures in the room.

➤ Forget traditional bathroom carpets such as those fuzzy bath mats. Go upscale and integrate this room with the rest of the house; the master bathroom should mimic the look, tone, and quality of the master bedroom.

➤ Add side mirrors on the vanity and a light above on the same wall and in the ceiling. Consider adding a light fixture above the shower.

➤ In a smaller bathroom where space is limited, eschew the glass tub enclosure in favor of a shower curtain. Doing so integrates the bath with the home and gives it a softer look; the curtain can be custom-made to coordinate with fabrics in the bedroom.

Glass between the shower and tub and on the exterior wall makes such a powerful design statement that nothing else needs to interfere.

This owner created a passage from an Old West saloon with this full-sized bar, which could be an added special space or a segment of the great room.

# DECORATING TIP—VIGNETTES:
# THE PUNCTUATION OF GOOD DESIGN

In her antiques-filled home in Wellesley, Massachusetts, Barbara Bent Hamilton, a Boston-area interior designer, created an odyssey of visual excitement with what she calls vignettes. Throughout the house, her décor has punch and excitement, and she has created it with a great deal more creativity than cash.

Hamilton advises, "Think of each vignette the way an artist composes a still-life painting or landscape. Just like the artist's painting, your real-life composition should be a mixture of height, volume, materials, and texture that all come into balance. At least three items are a pretty good way to start—definitely more than one."

Decide next where your "table scape" will go. A massive armoire that will be viewed from a distance can be topped with two or three antique suitcases arranged in a pleasing way. A nightstand benefits from something more intimate, such as a pair of grandma's glasses, a pocket watch, a miniature book, or a bud vase. Balance the composition with a good vignette or table scape. Go for impact, with elements such as luggage in different sizes and styles or by mixing different textures—natural fibers such as leather or basketry with a shiny piece of silver or brass work well together.

Found objects are a terrific way to start, and, says Hamilton, "While you cannot throw away your living room sofa on a whim, table scapes are meant to change with seasons or for holidays or whenever the mood strikes you." Even discarded items such as old books, kitchen utensils, or a single teacup are grist for Hamilton's visual mill.

continued...

...continued

Old trophies discarded by others—even sports equipment like a discarded lacrosse stick or a boat oar—can go in a living room and add impact. Collections, especially when they are of smaller items, are better displayed together. If you are a fan of pocket watches or thimbles, group the items in an antique-type box as a way of enhancing their impact. A collection of antique musical instruments can be distributed throughout the house and combined with other elements to tell a story.

"Think of your vignette as a work of art that has to meet the same criteria as a painting or sculpture or even a stage play. The element of surprise and the resolution of conflict are the cornerstones. For example, when you look at a table scape that includes pocket watches, you may want to surprise the viewer with elements that at first don't seem to belong, such as antique skeleton keys—because the keys are brass and the watches gold, they come together. Or perhaps, instead of displaying fruit in a bowl, display croquet balls," says Hamilton.

Photo © Brad Simmons

Nesting baskets atop an old chest and a tabletop that features interesting collections lend interest, charm, and personality to this room.

Bent-willow chairs with a throw are inviting on a cool morning or fall afternoon. Don't forget to include the porch when designing special spaces.

## Barbara Bent Hamilton:
## Table Scapes and Vignettes

➤ Plants and photographs go well when grouped together—especially if you have an outdoor photo twined with indoor foliage.

➤ Enliven dead areas such as mud rooms with something interesting; try using several different types of coat hooks or placing an antique pair of boots in the corner. Place mittens and gloves in an old milk crate or basket.

➤ Be resourceful. Display family photos, art collections, or children's artwork on the walls of a stairwell.

➤ Allow guests to participate. Keep out a sketch pad and invite guests to write or draw in it to record their experiences when weekending in your home. Occasionally frame their artwork—it will flatter your friends and your home.

➤ Go eclectic, mixing the old with the new—it creates interest and keeps costs down.

➤ If something is not aesthetically pleasing, put it away— that's what closets are for. Conversely, don't hide a unique tea set behind a closed door.

➤ Don't discard anything pretty or that may have sentimental value to your children.

*Nothing says Cape Cod like white, wicker, and natural cedar. Barbara Bent Hamilton advises, "Set out fun decorative items that your guests can use, like this straw hat with coordinating ribbon. Plenty of cut flowers are always welcome."*

Photo © Deck House, Inc.

➤ Old oriental rugs that are way past their useful lives can add elegance to a "nothing" area such as a mud room, laundry room, or extra bath. Hang them, or try turning them over—their back sides may have plenty of life left in them.

➤ Have fun. If you have a picture of your dog, hang it over his bowl at dog-eye level. There is no rule that says a well-designed home can't have a sense of humor.

➤ When you display books in a bookcase, pull them out to the edge of the shelves.

➤ Make your guest bedroom vignettes both useful and gender neutral. Keep out a basket of colorful towels and soaps. Fold beautiful blankets on top of a chest so overnight guests do not have to ask for them if they are cold.

"Shop for colorful fabric and make your own table-cloths for an inexpensive way to decorate for any season or occasion," says Barbara Bent Hamilton.

# Putting It All Together

In looking at this home, note which of the elements discussed so far have been put together under one roof. Through careful observation, you can almost see what the designer was thinking during the decorating process. This rural country home—built by Classic Post & Beam in LaGrange, Kentucky—is in perfect harmony with the horse-country estates surrounding it. Like most timberframe homes, this Classic home does not reveal its true elegance until you open the front door. This is when the house comes alive, revealing an open environment that leads your eye upward.

"Here in Kentucky we have beautiful weather and beautiful lawns—Kentucky bluegrass—so we wanted to reflect regional aesthetics," explains Jon Bednarski of Classic Post & Beam. Bednarski worked with Classic's design team in Maine to capture the Kentucky feeling for this home—including the cobblestone and cedar exterior, with gray-and-white trim that is typical of the region. "Considering the long warm seasons here, a

*This Classic Post & Beam home in the Louisville, Kentucky, area is an award winner of Homearama, which is held each year to showcase new and exciting houses and their interior décor. The traditional exterior gives little hint of the expansive open interior, save for the ample foyer window.*

173

patio and deck were imperative," says Bednarksi, who introduced this home as part of Homearama, an annual event that showcases the very best offered by Louisville-area architects, homebuilders, and interior designers.

When the interior of this home was created, it was designed to achieve the "wow!" factor and included using a lot of color to offset the wood posts and beams.

In addition, this home demonstrates that one need not be hamstrung by convention. As mentioned earlier, even though a timberframe home evokes a country or traditional style, you don't have to restrict yourself to that style. Timberframe construction provides a wonderful framework on which to build a warm and friendly atmosphere, but it does not necessarily limit your decorating style.

Notice the emphasis on bold and colorful elements. The mass of the beams provides the opportunity to use big furniture pieces and bold floral patterns in the rugs. Upholstered furniture has been combined with wicker. This keeps the informal tone and the relationship with the outdoors alive.

Inside, visitors arrive by way of the spacious foyer. This is the perfect area for greeting guests without making them feel crowded or forcing them to rush off to another room. Just off the foyer is a powder room with a pedestal sink. While every room has a touch of whimsy, the carved wooden Dalmatian in the foyer is the entry's humorous touch, as well as a nice conversation piece. The height of the foyer creates a natural, spacious feeling. The bronze look of the grille in the window is very effective, and grass and plants were used to complement the entry and integrate it with the outdoors.

Above the door, a large Palladian window frames the view and lets in a tremendous amount of light. At night, light emanating from this window makes the house seem friendly and inviting, especially when entertaining.

The window treatment
surrounding a traditional
fireplace gives this setting
an understated elegance.
Note how the formal
window treatment is offset
with informal metal and
wicker furniture.

*A tall piece of furniture such as an armoire balances the high ceiling and serves a multitude of purposes that can include additional storage for games or hiding a TV. In Europe and Asia, armoires are often the only closet space available for hanging clothes.*

The great room features a stone fireplace, a beamed vaulted ceiling to the ridge line of the roof, two skylights, a ceiling fan, and a thirty-four-by-ten-foot deck. The master bedroom and bath are also on the main floor. The two-story great room seemed to need grounding, or counterweight and balance to the soaring and expansive visual weight of the ceilings. The heavy-dimension timbers and the wood-paneled vault, if not compensated for, could have an overbearing presence. Balance was accomplished with the use of a large area rug with lots of design and color. Fabrics with a heavy texture, pattern, or color are an effective counterweight to the dominating presence of the beams overhead.

Upstairs features the second full bath and two additional bedrooms, each with a large under-eaves closet. Light pours onto the second-floor balcony through the foyer's large window.

The modest kitchen blends style and utility and includes a dishwasher, disposal, refrigerator, pantry, built-in range, wine rack, and self-cleaning oven. The breakfast area overlooks the deck. The kitchen was kept modest and an overpowering woodsy look avoided by using white cabinets and appliances. The kitchen floor is a wood laminate that extends into the dining nook, and the countertops are a versatile synthetic with an attractive stone look.

This ample Palladian window overlooks an expansive Kentucky bluegrass lawn typical of the area. Note how a sharp-edged high shelf is softened with the use of silk plants, which are ideal for hard-to-reach places. There is also a back-lit stained-glass window on the shelf to add a touch of opalescence. The wood Dalmatian adds amusement.

177

In keeping with the natural-elements motif throughout the home, a hooked area rug with fresh-fruit designs was chosen. A well-worn table and bright colors on the chair seats counter the white cabinetry.

In the master bedroom, muted leaf designs in the bed covering complement the potted plants. The leaf designs in the framed wall art here and throughout the home also extend the natural-elements motif. A flat-weave rug with floral patterns was used and a simple window treatment was chosen to avoid obscuring the view.

Oriental rugs are versatile, and they give an upscale look to a wood-accented home. Oriental rugs were used in the master bedroom, master bath, dining nook, and upstairs bedrooms.

The color choices complement the color of the wood. Yellows worked well with the natural yellow tones of the unstained timber, and natural fibers also worked well with the texture. For example, the sisal-look carpeting, wood look on the floors, and the wicker, rattan, and painted or natural-wood furniture complement the wood throughout the house. The natural motif is repeated with grasses, cattails, and other simple "plantings" in the urns and vases throughout the house.

*This attractive kitchen is relatively small and designed with modestly priced cabinets and appliances for a family that is on the go and spends little time on meal preparation.*

## DESIGN IDEAS YOU CAN LEARN FROM THIS HOME

➤ Bring out the beauty and warmth of natural-wood posts and beams with contrasting colors and textures.

➤ Accent open spaces, such as rooms with cathedral ceilings, with a few large pieces of furniture.

➤ Just as big pieces of furniture work well in expansive areas, big pieces of artwork look better on large walls. Smaller art objects should be saved for more intimate areas, such as bathrooms and hallways. Large pieces make a large wall come alive visually. By making large prints, paintings, and tapestries the focus, you can match furniture with the colors in the artwork more easily. The result is a strong, coordinated look for your living space.

➤ Pay careful attention to your lighting. Plan your lighting during the building stages so that wiring and electrical boxes can be put into place ahead of time. If you are undecided about having a fixture in a specific area, have the wiring and a box with a cap installed. This gives you flexibility and is more economical than wiring after you move in. Consider floor-up lighting. It's another way to light a space and fill in the dark spots that lurk around furniture and in corners.

continued...

These bentwood chairs were found at an antiques mall for under $200 and were re-covered in fabric identical to the window treatment. It is the kind of unexpected juxtaposition of elements that makes the environment interesting. The cushions are accented with flowers for unity. The bold pattern of the carpet coordinates perfectly with the walls.

Right: When a master bath leads directly into the master bedroom, consider a more upscale formal wall covering and an oriental rug to unify the tone of the two rooms. Notice that the fixtures are hidden from view when the door is open.

Lower Right: Go ahead—break the rules. Lots of people wouldn't think of placing their bed against the window, but here the scale of the window is a perfect fit. A bench at the foot of the bed finishes the look and provides a place for an early riser to sit down without disturbing his/her mate.

Photo © Jim Battles, Classic Post & Beam

...continued

➤ For window treatments and upholstery, florals and geometrics in bold colors are terrific. As a contrast, consider sheer white curtains to diffuse bright sunlight while adding warmth and comfort.

➤ Put the most durable rugs you can afford in the areas with heavier traffic—like stairs and foyers. When considering floor coverings, avoid clichés. Instead of a commonplace braided rug, try an oriental, a hooked, or an Aubusson-style rug.

➤ As with carpeting, countertops and flooring take a lot of abuse. If you install quality materials when you move in, they will look wonderful now and for as long as you own your home.

➤ When making budget decisions, determine the scope of the project first. Prioritize your needs room by room, then price each item accordingly. Obviously, if you decide to spend more on one item, you will have to spend less on another. Planning the overall project enables you to earmark funds for a few luxury items that you will cherish.

➤ Seek balance. And above all, make designing your place a journey with a destination that is fun, beautiful, personally gratifying, and full of pleasant surprises.

Photo © Jim Battles, Classic Post & Beam

# Resources

## Architects

Anmahian Winton Associates, Inc.
147 Sherman Street, Suite 107
Cambridge, MA 02140
617-497-6600
617-497-6611 fax
mail@annahian-winton.com

Duo Dickinson
94 Bradley Rd.
Madison, CT 06443
203-245-0405

Danny Eagan Architect, Inc.
Danny Eagan
70 North Center Street
P.O. Box 4896
Jackson Hole, WY 83001
307-733-8821
307-733-8652 fax
Danny/DEA@RMISP.com

## Bibliography

Gregorian, John B.
*Oriental Rugs of the Silk Route: Culture Process and Selection.*
New York: Rizzoli International Publications, Inc., 2000.
www.atgregorian.com

Morris, Michael, and Dick Pirozzolo.
*Timberframe Plan Book.*
Salt Lake City: Gibbs Smith, Publisher, 2000.

Washburn, Harry, and Kim Wallace.
*Why People Don't Buy Things.*
Reading: Perseus Books, 2000.

## Books

Bugg, Carol Donayre.
*Divine Design, 25th Anniversary Collection.*
Montgomery Village: Judd Publications, Inc., 1994.

Bugg, Carol Donayre.
*Smart & Simple Decorating.*
New York: Time-Life Books, 1999.

Douglas, Murray, Chippy Arvine (Contributor), and Albert Hadley (Introduction).
*Brunschwig & Fils Style.*
Boston: Bulfinch Press, 1995.

George, Judy, and Todd Lyon.
*The Domain Book of Intuitive Home Design: How to Decorate Using Your Personality Type.*
New York: Clarkson Potter, 1998.

Kylloe, Ralph.
*Rustic Style.*
New York: Harry N. Abrams, 1998.

O'Leary, Ann S., Gary R. Hall (Photographer), and Elizabeth Folwell (Introduction).
*Adirondack Style.*
New York: Clarkson Potter, 1998.

Walker, Daniel S.
*Flowers Underfoot:*
*Indian Carpets of the Mughal Era.*
New York: Metropolitan Museum of Art, 1997.

## Catalogs and Gift Centers

Shop@AOL
www.shopping.aol.com
Styleclick.com

## Interior Design Consultants

J/Brice Design International
326 A Street
Boston, MA 02210
617-695-9456
JORNS9456@jbricedesign.com

Decorating Den Interiors
19100 Montgomery Village Avenue
Montgomery Village, MD 20886
800-332-3367

Barbara Bent Hamilton Interiors
646 Worcestor Road
Wellesley, MA 02481
781-237-2866

## Internet Sites for Advice and Information

Art Prints
www.art.com

Better Homes and Gardens
www.bhg.com
www.decoratetoday.com

Decorating Den
www.decoratingden.com

Susan C. Druding,
international authority on fabrics
www.quilting.about.com
www.gazoontite.com

Home and Garden Television
www.hgtv.com

Interior World
www.interiorworld.com

Lynette Jennings
www.lynettejennings.com
She is one of North America's best-loved
authorities on home renovation, decorating,
and design. She is a former editor-in-chief of
*Select Homes and Food Magazine*, Canada's
leading monthly home and food publication.

## Lighting

GE Lighting North America
800-327-0533
www.gelighting.com/na/home

Osram Sylvania
100 Endicott Street
Danvers, MA 01923
800-544-4828
www.osramsylvania.com

## Magazine Resources

*Old House Journal*
Two Main Street
Gloucester, MA 01930
978-283-3200

*Timber Frame Homes Magazine*
Home Buyer Publications
4200-T Lafayette Center Drive
Chantilly, VA 20151
800-826-3893
www.timberframehomes.com

*Timber Frame Illustrated Magazine*
GCR Publishing
419 Park Avenue South, 18th Floor
New York, NY 10016
800-442-1869
212-245-1241 fax

## Organizations

Timber Frame Business Council
P.O. Box B1161
Hanover, NH 03755
603-643-5033

Timber Framers Guild
P.O. Box 60
Beckett, MA 01223
888-453-0879
www.tfguild.org
info@tfguild.com
Joel McCarty—joel@tfguild.com
Will Beemer—will@tfguild.com

## Timberframe and Post & Beam Companies

Bear Creek Timberwrights
1934 Middle Bear Creek Rd.
P.O. Box 335
Victor, MT 59875
406-642-6003
406-642-6005 fax
www.bearcreektimber.com

# Resources continued

The Cascade Joinery
1401 Sixth Street
Bellingham, WA 98225
Ross Grier
360-527-0119
360-527-0142 fax
www.cascadejoinery.com
info@cascadejoinery.com
Complete design services; frame fabrication
and installation; SIP enclosure.
Market Area: Worldwide

Classic Post & Beam
P.O. Box 546
York, ME 03909
Contact: James Nadeau
800-872-2326
207-363-2411 fax
www.classicpostandbeam.com
info@classicpostandbeam.com

Davis Frame Co.
P.O. Box 1079, Rte 12A
South Claremont, NH 03743
800-636-0993
603-543-0993 fax

Deck House, Inc.
930 Main Street
Acton, MA 01720
800-727-3325
www.deckhouse.com

Dreaming Creek Timber Frame Homes
2487 Judes Ferry Rd.
Powhatan, VA 23139
Robert Shortridge
804-598-4328
804-598-3748 fax
www.dreamingcreek.com
DCTFH@aol.com

Habitat Post & Beam
21 Elm Street S.
Deerfield, MA 01373
800-992-0121
413-665-4008 fax
www.postandbeam.com

HearthStone
1630 East Highway 25-70
Dandridge, TN 37725
Carmen Capio
865-397-9425
865-397-9262 fax
www.hearthstonehomes.com
ccaprio@hearthstonehomes.com

Lamore Lumber Post & Beam
Routes 5 and 10
Deerfield, MA 01342
413-773-8388
413-773-3188 fax

Lindal Cedar Homes, Inc.
P.O. Box 24426
Seattle, WA 98124
800-426-0536
www.Lindal.com

Maine Post & Beam of Cape Cod
78 Route
Sandwich, MA 02563
508-833-3111

Mountain Construction
Enterprises, Inc.
P.O. Box 1177
Boone, NC 28607
Mark Kirkpatrick
828-264-1231
828-264-4863 fax
www.mountainconstruction.com
mtnconst@boone.net

The Murus Company
P.O. Box 220
Route 549
Mansfield, PA 16933
Linda Lee
570-549-2100
570-549-2101 fax
www.murus.com
murus@epix.net
Structural insulated panels.

New Energy Works Timberframers
Housewrights & Joiners
1180 Commercial Drive
Farmington, NY 14425
800-486-0661
716-924-9962 fax
www.newenergyworks.com

Normerica Building Systems Inc.
150 Ram Forest Rd.
Gormely, ON L0H 1G0 Canada
Sam Kewen, Sales Manager
800-361-7449
905-841-9061 fax
www.normerica.com
info@normerica.com

Oakbridge Timber Framing
20857 Earnest Road
Howard, OH 43028
John Miller or Jim Kanagy
740-599-5711

Riverbend Timber Framing
P.O. Box 26
Blissfield, MI 49228
Frank Baker
517-486-4355
517-486-2056 fax
www.riverbendtf.com
Frank@rtfgli.clrs.com
Timber frames and panel-engineered packages,
timberframe erection, panel installation.
Market Area: National/International

George Senerchia Barn
Restorations and Timberframes
109 Old Post Road
Northford, CT 06472
203-484-2129

Jack A. Sobon, Timberframer
P.O. Box 201
Windsor, MA 01270
413-684-3223

Timbercraft Homes, Inc.
85 Martin Rd.
Port Townsend, WA 98368
Charles Landau
360-385-3051
360-385-7745 fax
www.timbercraft.com
info@timbercraft.com

Timberpeg
P.O. Box 5474
W. Lebanon, NH 03784
Bob Best
603-298-8820
603-298-5425 fax
www.timberpeg.com
info@timberpeg.com

Vermont Timberframes
7 Pearl St.
Cambridge, NY 12816
Tom Harrison
518-677-8860
518-677-3626 fax
www.vtf.com
tomharrison@vtf.com

Vermont Timber Works
P.O. Box 856
Springfield, VT 05156
Doug Friant, Dan Kelleher,
and Kimberly Morse
802-885-1917
802-885-6188 fax
www.VermontTimberWorks.com

Yankee Barn Homes
131 Yankee Barn Rd.
Grantham, NH 03753
Rob Knight
800-258-9786
603-863-4551 fax
www.yankeebarnhomes.com
info@yankeebarnhomes.com